Praise for

TURNING MYTHS INTO MONEY:
An Insider's Guide to Winning the Real Estate Game

Having been involved in the real estate industry for 19 years, I can tell you that Richard Steinhoff's book is invaluable for buyers, sellers and investors. He provides tips and insider information to help anyone with an interest in investing in real estate.

—**Greg Salter**, Director, Pacific Mortgage Funding Corporation

One of the greatest gifts real estate professionals can bestow upon clients and customers is to educate them on how to become successful in achieving their dreams when buying and selling real estate. In a time when education and knowledge are truly the 'key to the kingdom', **Turning Myths into Money: An Insider's Guide to Winning the Real Estate Game** *outlines in simple, easy to understand terms how to successfully maneuver in today's market.*

—**Edith Elzie**, Broker, Charlotte, NC

Having known Richard Steinhoff for about 30 years, I can attest to his integrity and depth of knowledge. He represented me in several real estate transactions. Richard knows the business inside and out. Listen to him and you will be better prepared to deal with this market.

—**Ed Hughes**, Vice-President Unilever, Retired

A three-decade career in real estate says it all: character. Richard Steinhoff is a role model for all those who represent buyers and sellers with the highest ethical standards. If you have any interest in real estate, you have to read **Turning Myths into Money: An Insider's Guide to Winning the Real Estate Game**.

—**Tony Winkle**, Former Executive Officer,
Orange County Board of Realtors, Sedona, AZ

Real estate is the largest purchase anyone makes in their lifetime and yet we buy homes or income property on our own or see a listing not knowing if the agent is reputable or not. Richard Steinhoff is the professionals, professional and now has written a book that is an essential read; everyone needs a copy in their library.

—**Ralph Rodham**, President, Rodham Marketing Group

Richard Steinhoff has utilized his 30 years of experience to create a valuable resource not only for buyers and sellers, but investors as well. I can attest from personal experience that he really knows what he is talking about.

—**Kristine Weatherly,** CFO, Spectrum Mechanical, Inc.

In this era of confusing and disastrous real estate scenarios, Richard Steinhoff manages to de-mystify the chaos and offer real-world solutions. In clear, sometimes humorous prose, he presents alternatives to foreclosure, ways to preserve home equity, and strategies that offer a way out of seemingly impossible dilemmas. If I ever had a serious real-estate problem, I'd go straight to Steinhoff's book for answers.

—**Maralys Wills**, Author of, *Damn the Rejections, Full Speed Ahead: The Bumpy Road to Getting Published.*

Richard Steinhoff has written the book that all realtors talk of dispelling the Myths and seeking the truths about buying and selling real estate, and that could only be written by someone with many years in the business. A must read for everyone.

—**Kathy Martin**, Realtor, Northport, NY

Richard Steinhoff has penned an invaluable and current real estate classic. Agents, buyers and sellers will appreciate this 'guide book' to direct us through the current minefield of economic, financial and transactional pitfalls prevalent in this marketplace. Richard brings decades of experience and direct knowledge that only comes with successfully serving clients through multiple real estate cycles. Buy this book—read it—and gift it to anyone in the market that you care about!

—**Jay Rodgers**, Realtor, St. Louis, MO

This book is crammed with a wealth of information and it will become required reading for anyone in the real estate field. There is enough detail to guide you through the maze of the real estate business. It is clearly written, easy to read and understand.

—**C. Gene Kullmann**, Real Estate Investor, San Diego, CA

Yes indeed, the current real estate market is a 'mine field.' Richard Steinhoff provides some great advice and insight from the perspective of a 30-year career professional.

—**Bill Stewart**, Broker Owner, Provident Real Estate, Novato, CA

At the pace that real estate purchasing and selling is changing in today's world, it is increasingly more important for buyers and sellers to have a comprehensive understanding of the process. In **Turning Myths into Money: An Insider's Guide to Winning the Real Estate Game**, *Richard Steinhoff provides a wonderful resource for understanding this process."*

—**Larry Spurgeon**, Real Estate Specialist/Consultant, Austin, TX

Richard Steinhoff's book will help both beginners and experienced real estate investors profit in today's challenging markets. New market strategies such as investing in foreclosures and short sales will enable the reader to profit in both up and down real estate markets. Also, the novice investor will learn how to benefit and cut losses just like the pros when a real estate purchase starts to decline.

—**Steven J. Williams**, Certified Financial Planner, Santa Monica, CA

Richard Steinhoff has put together a great resource including a very timely topic that everyone who is even thinking about buying or selling real estate in the next few years needs to know about: short sales. Richard deconstructs many of the current Myths regarding short sales and he does it with facts bound in real life stories you can relate to. A great resource to get clear on a very cloudy subject.

—**Joe Curtis**, President, Pickford Escrow, San Diego, CA

Finally a step-by-step guide to our present day real estate market. This book should help answer those many unanswered questions.

—**Lynette Montoya**, President, Global Hotel Partners, Inc., Santa Fe, NM

TURNING MYTHS into MONEY

An Insider's Guide to WINNING *the Real Estate Game*

H. Richard STEINHOFF

NEW YORK

TURNING MYTHS into MONEY

An Insider's Guide to WINNING the Real Estate Game

by H. Richard Steinhoff

ISBN 978-1-60037-942-0 Paperback
ISBN 978-1-60037-943-7 E-Pub Version
Library of Congress Control Number: 2011922088

Published by:

MORGAN JAMES PUBLISHING
The Entrepreneurial Publisher
5 Penn Plaza, 23rd Floor
New York City, New York 10001
(212) 655-5470 Office
(516) 908-4496 Fax
www.MorganJamesPublishing.com

Cover Design by:
Rachel Lopez
rachel@r2cdesign.com

Interior Design by:
Bonnie Bushman
bbushman@bresnan.net

In an effort to support local communities, raise awareness and funds, Morgan James Publishing donates one percent of all book sales for the life of each book to Habitat for Humanity.
Get involved today, visit
www.HelpHabitatForHumanity.org.

ACKNOWLEDGEMENTS

First and foremost, I want to thank my daughter, Lisa, who encouraged me for years to write a book. Once I started, you gave me inspired, creative ideas and sent me in a whole new direction with the manuscript. Without you, this book would never have happened. I am so grateful for you. I love you, Lisa.

I especially want to thank Maralys Wills for her friendship, her excellent advice on enhancing readability, and her superb critiques. You taught me so much. I will be forever grateful. Good job, Maralys.

I want express my appreciation to my publisher, Rich Frishman, for his support and sage advice. You were always there for me with an encouraging word during the very difficult times of the last six months. I couldn't have done it without you. Thank you, Rick.

I am truly grateful to David Hancock for the giving me the opportunity to become a published author and work with the very talented Morgan James staff.

I will never forget you, David. Thank you.

I want to thank Margo Toulouse, my Author Relations Manager, for guiding me through the Morgan James process. I don't know what I would have done without you. Thank you, Margo.

Thanks to Brian Buffini, my mentor and friend for the last 14 years, for placing Elaine and I on the right path, and keeping us there. You are always there when I need you. You have changed our lives, and I will always be grateful. Thank you, Brian.

My profound gratitude to my wife, Elaine, for standing by me during this process, as always, and for keeping me healthy enough to finish the job. You are truly amazing and I am so lucky to have you. All my love forever.

I want to thank Laurie Gibson for her brilliant editing and suggestions for improving the content. You are a true professional. Thank you, Laurie.

My thanks also go out to Jim Linehan from Microsoft. What an unbelievable job you did to guide me through the Microsoft Word program. You were amazing and Word is amazing. Thank you, Jim.

I also want to thank my entire family for supporting and encouraging me, not only on this project, but throughout my life. Thank you Lisa, Brian, Sydney, Rick, Mary Anne, Brittany, Michael, Ryan, Nina, Kevin, Cameron, Hailey, Hannah, Gabe, Debbie, Jerry, Kimberly, Josh, Kaitlyn, Diana, and Walter. I love you all.

Thanks to my good friend John McDermott for your support and excellent input. You are truly appreciated and I am lucky to have you as a friend.

I want to express my sincere appreciation to the following organizations for allowing me to share invaluable information from their websites:

- The National Association of Realtors, and Hilary Marsh
- The Real Estate Buyer's Agent Council, and Kristen Short
- Freddie Mac, and Brad German, Barbara Wise-Velez
- The U.S. Department of Housing and Urban Development
- The U.S. Department of the Treasury
- Pickford Escrow, and Joe Curtis, Rosie Poole
- California Title Company, and Jim Waterman, Cam Hunter
- California Association of Realtors, and Laura Williamson
- Fair Isaac Corporation, and Craig Watts
- Real Trends, Inc., and Doniece Welch
- First American Home Buyers Protection Corporation, and Jerilyn Milligan

Thank you all for your generous support.

A special thanks to author Robert Krantz for your sage advice.

Thanks to everyone who provided endorsements. You are all very special to me, and I am truly grateful.

FOREWORD

When looking for insight on the complexities of this new era of real estate, you won't find anyone more knowledgeable than Richard Steinhoff. His insight is based on real-world, practical experience. Richard has spent decades in the trenches, wrestling through the complexities that each real estate transaction now represents.

There are many so-called "experts" on TV, giving their opinion on real estate who've never actually walked anybody through a transaction, and they just don't have the depth or breadth of knowledge that Richard possesses.

If I had a friend or family member buying real estate in this market, I would want them to have a copy of *Turning Myths into Money: An Insider's Guide to Winning the Real Estate Game.*

Don't just read this book, digest it. Use it and make your real estate purchase or sale a lot smoother and much more profitable.

–**Brian Buffini**, Chairman and Founder,
Buffini and Company

CONTENTS

Section 3: Adventures in Short Sales

Section 4: Spotlight on Foreclosures

SECTION 5: The Art of Buying

INTRODUCTION

Real estate is one of the hottest topics in America today. You can't open a newspaper or magazine without seeing some kind of dramatic article. Real estate horror stories are constantly on television news programs. Millions of people are losing their homes to foreclosure or are resorting to a "short sale" because the value of their home is less than their mortgage.

Home prices have fallen over 30 percent. It is very difficult for buyers to obtain financing to purchase a home. People are in trouble and they need reliable information so they can make good decisions to protect their interests.

I decided to do something to help. Drawing on my 30 years of experience as a real estate broker, I wrote: *Turning Myths into Money: An Insider's Guide to Winning the Real Estate Game.* This is a "one-source" text filled with comprehensive information, tips, insider secrets, and real solutions to help you protect and build wealth. It covers every aspect of real estate—including buying, selling, financing, agent selection, and investing. It also covers the currently relevant topics of "short sales" and foreclosures. These topics are explored using 90 popular real estate Myths, separating fact from fiction.

Turning Myths into Money: An Insider's Guide to Winning the Real Estate Game was written for the 78 million homeowners in America, as well as the millions of people who will be buying a home in the future. I hope that the lessons learned from this book will help you make better decisions and win the real estate game.

H. Richard Steinhoff

www.hrichardsteinhoff.com

(Note: For the purpose of conciseness, I have used "he" throughout the book to represent both genders.)

Section 1:
ALL ABOUT AGENTS

No discussion about real estate would be complete without talking about real estate agents. The real estate agent's main job is to represent you in buying or selling property. You may love them or hate them, but they can be one of the best things that ever happened to you. A lot of misinformation exists about real estate agents, so we are going to give you the true picture from inside the industry. This section will clarify who agents are, what they do, how they get paid, and how they can help you. This will be done by exploring some popular Myths.

To become a real estate agent, you to have to pass a state-administered real estate examination and obtain a license to sell. Most states require some college-level courses prior to taking the exam. However, a college degree is not required. Almost all states require that the agent take some continuing education courses to renew his license, usually every four years.

Myth # 1: Female Agents are Superior to Male Agents

Fiction: According to the National Association of Realtors, 57 percent of their membership is female, and 43 percent male. NAR does not keep track of individual agent production, so we checked with Real Trends, Inc., and found that 6 of the top 10 producing agents in America were male, including the top 3, based on the number of transactions.[1] This doesn't mean that you need a male agent. It means that a top agent can be either male or female, so it should make no difference to you.

---

1   Real Trends, Inc. and The Wall Street Journal, used with permission

Myth # 2: Agents are Paid Salaries by Their Brokers

Fiction: Real estate agents are self-employed, independent contractors responsible for their own success or failure. They are also responsible for all their own expenses. Agents are compensated solely on a commission basis, not by salary. So if you don't buy or sell a house with them and close it, they don't get paid!

Myth # 3: All Agents are Realtors®

Fiction: In order to use the term "Realtor®", which is a trademark of the National Association of Realtors, an agent must pay to belong to the National Association of Realtors (NAR) and subscribe to their "Code of Ethics." Realtors are held to a higher standard than regular real estate agents. They also have access to a vast array of educational programs, research, and resources.

Buyers and sellers have recourse if they have a problem with a Realtor. A Professional Standards Committee has been established at the local level to handle complaints about Realtors. NAR was formed in 1908 and the "Code of Ethics" was adopted in 1913. As you can see, Realtors have been around for a long time.

The Code of Ethics is shown in Appendix A.

 TIP: Always Use a Realtor, Not Just an Agent, When Buying or Selling.

Myth # 4: Any Agent Can Broker a Transaction on His Own

Fiction: An agent must place his license under a real estate broker. Under agency law, the broker represents the principle in negotiating the sale of real property. As a practical matter, the agent usually negotiates the sale, but the broker is ultimately responsible and must approve and sign all contracts.

Myth # 5: I Need to Call Many Agents to See All the Houses That are Available

Fiction: In most areas, all homes that are listed for sale with agents are contained in a Multiple Listing Service (MLS), which is a paid subscription. All serious agents are members and have access to the same list, so there is no advantage in using multiple agents.

Myth # 6: Agents List for a Higher Price to Earn More Commission

Fiction: By raising the listing price, the agent's percentage of the difference is a very small amount. For example, if you raised the price by $10,000, the total commission would increase by $600, assuming a 6 percent commission. This is split equally between the listing and selling offices, which means your agent's office would receive $300. The agent's split averages 60 percent; therefore, the agent would receive only an additional $180. An agent who is trained and motivated to sell property would not risk his entire commission by overpricing a listing just to gain an additional $180. You can use larger numbers, but the differential is still small. A good agent will want to list your house at a price where it will sell, without considering how it affects the commission.

Myth # 7: An Agent Can Represent Only a Buyer or a Seller, Not Both

Fiction: According to NAR, a listing agent can represent both the buyer and the seller, but would then become a "Dual Agent."

There are three types of Agency:

Seller's Agent: Represents the seller only, and works in the seller's best interest. The agent can work with buyers as customers, but remains an agent of the seller. This means that the buyer doesn't have full representation—at least not from that agent.

Buyer's Agent: Represents the buyer only, and works in the buyer's best interest. This creates a more natural relationship with the buyer, and gives him full representation.

Dual Agent: Brokerage firm represents both buyer and seller in the same transaction, with the consent of both. This could involve one agent, or two agents if one represents the buyer and one represents the seller.

All agency relationships, regardless of type, must be disclosed in writing to all parties. Some states permit non-agency relationships with parties to a real estate transaction. Commonly known as a "Transaction Broker," he owes reduced duties to the parties because he doesn't represent either one.

 TIP: Always Have an Agent Representing Just You in a Transaction, Whether You are a Buyer or Seller.

Myth # 8: You Don't Need an Agent to Buy a House, It's All on the Internet

Fiction: All of the major real estate Internet sites such as www.realtor com and www.zillow.com will direct you to the listing agent to find out more about a house. So you see, you end up dealing with an agent anyway. But you may want to think twice about working directly with the listing agent. (See Myth # 9.)

Myth # 9: You Can Save Money by Buying a House Directly from the Listing Agent

Fiction: When you buy directly from the listing agent, he is the agent of the seller. All his loyalty is to the seller. His incentive is to get the highest price for his client. (In this situation, you have no representation.) He also receives the entire commission because there in is no selling agent. Even though he represents the seller, the agent still has to show good faith and deal honestly with the buyer.

Myth # 10: Agents Make Too Much Money for What They Do, They Have an Easy Job

Fiction: The agent's job is both complicated and demanding. It is one of the most stressful professions in America. Their responsibilities are endless and include:

For Sellers:

1. **Listing Price:** The agent will assist the seller in establishing a listing price. To accomplish this, the agent usually prepares a Comparative

Market Analysis (CMA), which includes analyzing homes on the market, recent sales, and expired listings.

2. **Staging**: The agent will help the seller "stage" the property so that it will be more attractive to potential buyers. This involves removing clutter, cleaning off countertops, rearranging closets, making minor repairs, rearranging furniture, and enhancing curb appeal.

3. **Marketing**: The agent will provide the seller with a marketing plan that will include advertising directly for buyers in the media, and indirectly by placing the properly in the Multiple Listing Service (MLS). The agent will conduct a "Caravan" from their office so that all the agents in that office can see the property. They will then hold a "Broker Preview" for all other agents in the area. They will place a sign and a lock box on the property to facilitate showings. They will also put the property on various Internet websites, such as www.realtor.com

4. **Disclosure:** The agent will educate the seller and ensure that the seller provides the buyer with all required disclosures.

5. **Negotiation:** On the seller's behalf, the agent will develop a strategy and conduct negotiations with buyers and their agents.

6. **Inspections and Repairs:** The agent will review all buyer inspection reports with the seller and assist in deciding which buyer requested repairs they should make.

7. **Closing:** The agent will monitor the buyer's contingencies for timely removal, coordinate with attorneys and/or escrow, and oversee the closing process to insure that everything goes smoothly.

For Buyers:

1. **Location:** The agent will help the buyer locate neighborhoods where he would like to live.

2. **Requirements:** The agent will assist the buyer in establishing his requirements for a house. These include price, size, number of bedrooms and baths, number of stories, size of garage, and other amenities.

3. **Find Properties**: The agent will search the MLS and other sources for properties that meet the buyer's requirements.

4. **Touring:** The agent will make an appointment with the buyer to show the properties he has found.

5. **Writing the Offer:** After finding a property that the buyers like, the agent will discuss and write an offer.

6. **Negotiation**: The agent will present the offer to the seller through the seller's agent and then negotiate the sale. Sometimes this involves one or more counter- offers from either or both parties.

7. **Reviewing Disclosures:** The agent will ensure that all required disclosures are received from the seller, and review those disclosures with the buyer.

8. **Inspections**: The agent will assist the buyer in scheduling inspections that the buyer requests. This may include a physical inspection, a termite inspection, a geological inspection, a roof inspection, a structural inspection, and an environmental inspection.

9. **Repairs**: The agent will send a repair request to the seller based on the buyer's analysis of the inspection reports.

10. **Closing**: The agent will assist the buyer in scheduling the final walk-through, and oversee the closing process to ensure that everything goes well.

A Realtor is on duty 24/7. Clients want to meet and look at properties or talk about listing their houses when the clients are not at work, usually nights and weekends. The rest of the time, the agent takes care of his other duties. It is truly one of the most difficult, demanding, and stressful jobs on the planet!

Myth # 11: You Must Pay Your Agent's Commission When You Sign a "Buyer Representation Agreement"

Fiction: When you sign a Buyer Representation Agreement, you are committing to buy a house from your agent who, in turn, commits to work diligently to find a house for you. With this signed document, the agent will work hard for you because you won't buy a house from another agent. This happens a lot when the agent doesn't have this document, and it is very discouraging for the agent. What the agreement says is you consent to pay your agent a commission if he finds a house you want to buy, but the fee will be offset by any amount received from the seller. However, it is a rare occurrence when the seller won't pay a commission. If the property is listed with an agent, the seller will pay the commission 99 percent of the time. The only time this could be an issue is when you find a "For Sale By Owner" (FSBO) house that you want to buy, and the owner will not pay a commission, or when the agent has a "pocket listing." This occurs when a house is not on the market, but the owner will sell for the right price.

 TIP: Don't Be Afraid to Sign a Buyer Representation Agreement Because the Chance of You Having to Pay a Commission is Almost a Non-Issue.

Marilyn was a single lady in her 30s.She was a nurse and earned a good income. When she came to us, she was pre-qualified and ready to buy a house. We suggested that Marilyn sign a Buyer Representative Agreement with our agent, Sally, who worked with first-time buyers.

Marilyn was comfortable with paying a commission to find the right house. She really wanted a new home, so Sally took her to all the new tracts in her price range. (Normally, builders in our area do not pay commissions, but with the bad economy, many were paying commissions to agents bringing qualified buyers.)

After Sally had taken her to see several resale homes, Marilyn decided that she really wanted a new home in one of the tracts she had seen. It was a townhome development, so the exterior maintenance was taken care of by the Homeowners Association. This was perfect for Marilyn because she worked long hours.

Sally took her back to the new tract, and Marilyn found a model that she fell in love with. She told Sally that this was the one, and she signed a Purchase Agreement with the builder. Then, with apprehension, she asked Sally how much commission she would have to pay. When Sally told her that the builder was paying the commission, and she would owe nothing on the Buyer Representation Agreement, Marilyn's eyes teared up, and she gave Sally a long, heartfelt hug.

Myth # 12: I Can Sell My House Myself and Save Thousands

Fiction: Very rarely can a homeowner sell a house on his own and end up with higher net proceeds than had he used an agent. To illustrate, in any given market, only about 10 percent of the homes for sale are being sold directly by owners. Why would a buyer pass up 90 percent of the homes on the market to buy directly from an owner?

The answer is, to save the commission and get a better price, but the seller is also trying to save the commission and get a better price.

Do you see the dilemma? As a matter of fact, 90 percent of "For Sale By Owners" end up listing their house with an agent. Also, a study by the National Association of Realtors found that houses sell for 3 percent to 9.5 percent more when sold through a Realtor.

 TIP: If You are Going to Sell Your House, Hire an Agent. Don't Even Think about Doing It Yourself.

Jim was a very competent aerospace engineer with many years of experience. When he was transferred to another city, he decided that he was smart enough to market his house himself, thereby saving thousands of dollars that he would normally pay a real estate agent. He decided not to put a sign in his yard because he didn't want his neighbors to know he was selling. He did, however, run an ad in the local newspaper. The response was mostly from real estate agents looking for a listing, so Jim started holding open houses on the weekends.

During the very first open house, a nice couple came by. While the husband talked to Jim, his wife took a tour of the house. Later, after he closed up for the day, Jim went into the bedroom to change clothes. That's when he discovered that his watch, rings, wallet, and some cash were all missing. He was shocked that someone would take advantage of him like that.

After a month of open houses, a man came by on a Sunday and decided that he wanted to buy the house. They sat down at the kitchen table to work out the terms of the sale. The man, we will call Charley, said he knew the house had been on the market for a while, which meant that the price was too high. Plus, he said, Jim was going to save $36,000 in commissions. (Jim was asking $600,000.) Charley said the most he would pay was $500,000. Jim replied that the best he could do was $575,000. Charley countered back at $540,000, which he said was his final offer. By now, Jim was tired of the drudgery of selling, so he accepted the offer of $540,000. His commission savings were now gone, plus a lot more.

It didn't end there. After the 60-day closing date passed, Jim asked Charley when he was going to close. Charley told him the lender needed more information from him, so there would be a delay in the closing date. Jim found out who the lender was and called to find out the status of Charley's loan. He was told that Charley couldn't qualify for the loan to buy his house. Jim had just lost another 60 days.

It was now four months since he started selling his home, and his employer was pressing him to move. Reluctantly, Jim called one of our agents to list his house. It sold in two weeks, and closed 45 days later at $590,000.

This was a good lesson for Jim. He could have saved all that time, plus, he lost some valuable possessions. Also, by paying his agent's fee, he ended up with a much better price, which more than covered the commission.

Myth # 13: The Only Way to Find a Good Agent is to Check Ads in Local Real Estate Magazines

Fiction: There are several methods used to find a good agent, including this one.

Method 1: Check ads in local real estate publications

Look at ads in local real estate publications and see which agents are prominent in the area where you are interested. Call the agents and arrange a meeting.

Method 2: Check local "For Sale" signs

Drive around the area where you want to live and make a note of the names and phone numbers on the "For Sale" signs. Call the agents to arrange interviews.

Method 3: Check the Internet

Look on real estate websites, such as www.realtor.com and www.zillow.com to find out which agents are active in the area you are interested in. Then call the agent and arrange an interview.

Method 4: Check Mailers

This is mainly for sellers, because they will be receiving mail from agents at their house. The same thing applies. Call the most active agents and make an appointment to interview them.

Method 5: Check Local Offices

Visit local real estate offices serving the area where you want to buy or sell. It is better to go with a franchise office or a large, regional independent. The real estate franchise companies generally have a higher standard for their agents in terms of training and quality. The offices usually divide the hours they are open into four-hour segments, and assign a different agent for each time slot. The agent's job is to talk to people who walk in or call, and convert them to clients. This is called "Floor Time." You want a good top agent, but the odds are that person will not be the one on duty. Top agents are usually too busy for floor time. To find out who they are, talk to the manager. Ask the manager which agents are most active in your area, and who will be most compatible with you. Then make an appointment to interview that person. If you are not satisfied with the first one, ask to see another. Sometimes you might have to go to another office to find the right agent.

 TIP: Don't Just Take the Agent on Duty

Interviewing Agents: Try to establish rapport with the agent by asking personal questions. Ask about his sales record and how long he has been selling real estate. The bottom line is that you need to have a good feeling about that person.

Method 6: The Best Method: Referral

Whether you are a buyer or seller, the best way to select a good agent is the same way you select a doctor, dentist, or hair stylist. You get a referral! Ask around. Ask your friends, your neighbors, your relatives, your co-workers, and your service providers.

People have received good agent referrals from their insurance agents, their financial advisors, their attorneys, and their stockbrokers. Someone you know will surely have had a good experience with a real estate agent. That way, you have the opportunity to work with an agent who has a good track record with an acquaintance, and who wants to maintain a good reputation by taking great care of you. In addition to the commission, the agent's incentive is to do well so that he will receive more referrals from your friends—and maybe even from you!

 TIP: Make Sure That You Get a Full-Time Agent So He Can Devote Enough Time to Accomplish Your Real Estate Goals.

Ralph had just been transferred to our area and needed to find a house for his family. He was married with two small children, so he needed a community with good schools and a low crime rate. He had been pre-approved for a loan of $400,000 by a lender that worked with his company. He also had $120,000 for a down payment from the sale of his previous home.

The first thing he did was to call on an ad that he saw in the newspaper. He met with the agent, and told him that the most he wanted to pay for a house was $500,000. The agent proceeded to show him homes in the $600,000 to $700,000 price range. When Ralph asked why, the agent said that all prices were negotiable.

This didn't sit well with Ralph, so he called on another ad, and met with a second agent. This time, the agent said that he would check the listings, put together a tour, and get back to him to set up an appointment. One week later, he hadn't heard back from that agent, so he called and left him a message. Another three days passed with no contact from the agent.

Frustrated, Ralph told one of his co-workers about his dilemma. The co-worker told him that when he moved here, he worked with an agent from our office who was very competent and listened to his needs. She was a delight to work with and found him a house that satisfied all his requirements. Her name was Barbara, and he would be happy to give Ralph her contact information.

Ralph called Barbara, and she found him a house right away that more than met all his needs. He was ecstatic! After the sale closed, Ralph gave Barbara a gift certificate to a very exclusive day spa to show his appreciation.

A good, competent Realtor can be invaluable to both buyers and sellers. You can find one fairly easily by obtaining a referral from someone you know. Whether you are buying, selling, or investing, you should seriously consider working with a real estate professional.

You'll be glad you did; they can save you time, money, and a lot of worry!

Section 2:
SHOW ME THE MONEY

The availability of financing for home purchases is a wondrous thing! By providing buyers with the ability to obtain a home loan, real estate lenders have performed a great service for the American people, because few of them could pay cash.

This section will cover all aspects of financing a home, including how lending works, the loan process, and types of available loans. It will provide tips on lender selection, how to decide which loan is best, and how much of a down payment to make.

Myth # 14: It's Best to Wait until You Can Pay Cash before Buying a House

Fiction: If it were necessary to pay cash, buying a home would be totally out of reach for most people. With today's prices, can you imagine how long it would take to save enough to pay cash? Besides, most people can use a tax write-off. Since the government allows you to deduct the interest paid on your mortgage and your property tax on your tax return, why not take advantage of this break?

Myth # 15: I Need to Be Pre-Qualified for a Loan before Making an Offer

Fiction: This used to be the norm, but in today's world, it is essential to be pre- approved for a loan, not just pre-qualified, before you go shopping for a home. If you are going to buy a short sale or a bank-owned property, this is especially true. Banks have little tolerance for buyers making an offer without a pre-approved loan. You can see why. On a pre-qualification, the lender normally does not verify income or down payment and it is no guarantee of a loan. The bank, therefore, does not know whether or not they have a real buyer, and does not want to waste time finding out.

Jeff and Cory were a married couple in their 30s. They both worked and had a good joint income. They had no children, but were ready to start a family. They were referred to our agent, Joan, who suggested strongly that they obtain a pre-approval letter from a lender. They met with a lender, and were approved for a loan of $385,000 and had $40,000 to put down. Joan started showing them neighborhoods. After several outings, they found a neighborhood that suited all their needs, so Joan narrowed her search to that area.

After looking at several homes, they selected one that was bank owned. When Jane contacted the listing agent, she was told that there were already six offers on the property. Jeff and Cory told Joan that they really wanted this house, and asked what they needed to do to make that happen.

The house was listed for $420,000. Joan told them to draw up an offer for $425,000, which was their maximum, and to request a closing time of 15 days. Even though one of the other offers was for $430,000, the bank accepted Jeff and Cory's offer because they were the only buyers who were pre-approved and could close fast, saving the bank money.

Jeff and Cory were grateful they had listened to Joan.

Myth # 16: When Shopping for a Loan, Always Take the One with the Best Interest Rate

Fiction: The interest rate on a loan is important, but not as important as the Annual Percentage Rate (APR). The APR shows you the total cost of the loan, including points and fees paid to the lender to obtain the loan. The lowest interest rate may not be the most cost effective.

For example, let's compare a $200,000 loan at 5.0 percent fixed interest rate, amortized over 30 years, with 1.25 points (a point is 1 percent of the loan amount), to the same loan at 5.25 percent with no points. The monthly payment on the first loan would be $1,074, and on the second loan $1,104, a difference of $30. With a loan fee of $2,500, it would take almost seven years at $30 per month before you equaled the $2,500 you would have paid up front on the first loan.

So you see, the lower interest rate loan doesn't make sense if you are not planning to live in the house for more than seven years.

 TIP: *When Obtaining a Loan, Always Check the APR, Not Just the Interest Rate*

Myth # 17: It's Always Best to Get a Fixed Rate Loan

Fiction: There are two basic types of housing-related loans, Fixed Rate Mortgages and Adjustable Rate Mortgages (a mortgage is a loan secured by a home). On a fixed rate mortgage, the monthly payment stays the same for the entire term of the loan, usually 15 or 30 years. On an adjustable rate mortgage (ARM), the monthly payment will change at specific times. The interest rate is based on an economic index that will move up or down over the term of the loan.

The ARM is usually fixed for an initial period, typically 6 to 12 months. At the end of the initial period, and at every subsequent adjustment period, the interest rate adjusts based on two factors, the index and the margin. For example, a loan based on the 11th District Cost of Funds Index (COFI), which is currently 3.25 percent, plus a margin of 1.25 percent, will create an interest rate of 4.5 percent. As the index increases or decreases, your payment will change with it.

All ARMs also have rate caps that regulate how much the interest rate can change at each adjustment point, and lifetime ceiling and floor rates. To illustrate, using a base rate of 4.5 percent in the above example, a typical ARM could adjust up or down no more than 2.0 percent in each succeeding 12-month period, and have a lifetime ceiling of 9.5 percent, and a floor rate of 2.5 percent over the life of the loan.

Lenders sometimes use ARMs with a teaser rate, which is a rate significantly lower than the market rate, to entice you. In our example, the teaser rate might be 2.5 percent, but it would go up to 4.5 percent at the end of the teaser period, usually 6 months. (You still have to qualify at the higher note rate.)

There are several common indexes that are used for ARMs, as seen in Figure 2.1.

There is another form of ARM called a Hybrid Adjustable Rate Mortgage. This ARM is fixed for an initial period, anywhere from 3 to 10 years, and then the interest rate adjusts like a regular ARM for the remainder of the loan.

There is also a rarely used mortgage called a Balloon/Reset Mortgage. It's a loan that begins with a fixed rate for a period of 5 or 7 years, for example, and amortized over 30 years. After the initial period, you then have the option of resetting the loan to the current market rate or paying it off. This loan is more commonly used for commercial properties and is best for buyers who don't expect to live in the home beyond the initial fixed-rate period.

Who Should use a Fixed Rate Loan?

Fixed rate mortgages are a good choice for first-time buyers, people on a fixed income, or people who plan to keep their home for a very long time.

Who Should use an ARM?

ARMs are good for people with upward mobility or for people who plan to move in a relatively short period. Also, because the initial interest rate on an ARM is usually lower than a fixed rate mortgage, you can qualify for a larger loan.

 TIP: If You are Using an ARM to Purchase a Home, Make Sure You Can Afford the Payment When the Interest Rate Increases, Especially with a Teaser Rate Loan.

Figure 2.1: Common ARM Indexes

1. **One-Year Treasury Bill**
   Based on the rate of return of the one-year U.S. Treasury Bill.

2. **London Interbank Offered Rate (LIBOR)**
   Based on the average interest rate at which banks in the London Interbank Market borrow funds from each other.

3. **Cost of Funds Index (COFI)**
   Based on the weighted average of the cost of funds for the Federal Home Loan Bank in San Francisco (11th District Cost of Funds index)

Myth # 18: Your Credit Score is Important When Applying for a Loan

Fact: If you are thinking about buying a house, there is one number you need to pay close attention to: your credit score. It not only determines how much money you can get on a loan, but also the terms of your loan. Scores run from 300 to 850. The higher your score, the better interest rate you will receive, as shown in Figure 2.2. As you can see, the difference in monthly payment between a score of 620 and 760 is almost $300 on a $300,000 mortgage.

The credit score was developed by the Fair Isaac Corporation, hence FICO® score. The FICO® score predicts the probability of your becoming 90 days late on an account in the next two years. Fair Isaac develops three credit scores, one for each of the credit bureaus: Experian, TransUnion, and Equifax. The scores will differ slightly between the bureaus, mainly because they each may have different credit items reported to them. Also, you could have credit under different names, which would affect your scores differently.

The FICO® score is widely used by mortgage lenders, as well as Fannie Mae and Freddie Mac. The Federal National Mortgage Corporation (Fannie Mae) and the Federal Home Loan Mortgage Corporation (Freddie Mac) are both government-sponsored, shareholder-owned enterprises charted by Congress to provide a continuous flow of funds for residential mortgages. They accomplish this by buying residential mortgages from lenders that meet their criteria and issuing mortgage-backed securities, which they sell to investors. This process provides lenders with new funds for homebuyers.

Fannie Mae and Freddie Mac do not make loans directly to consumers.

Figure 2.2: Credit Score Effects on Monthly Payment[2]
(Based on a $300,000 mortgage)

FICO ® Score	APR	Monthly Payment
760–850	4.202%	$1,467
700–759	4.424%	$1,507
680–699	4.601%	$1,538
660–679	4.815%	$1,577
640–659	5.245%	$1,656
620–639	5.791%	$1,759

According to www.myFICO.com, the following factors determine your credit score:[3]

1. Your payment history

2. Amount of debt you owe

3. How long you have been using credit

4. How often you have applied for new credit

5. The types of credit you currently use

If you know your credit score and want to see how you compare to other people, look at Figure 2.3. If you don't know your score, you can obtain it at www.myFICO.com. There are many ways to improve your credit score, some of which are outlined in Figure 2.4.

There is also a new generation of FICO score, developed specifically to enhance its ability to predict consumer credit risk. It is known as the FICO 8 score. Below are the major differences from the previous version:

---

2 Reprinted with permission of www.myFICO.com
3 Reprinted with permission of www.myFICO.com

1. It is more sensitive to highly used credit cards. If your card has a balance close to the limit, you will probably lose more points than before.

2. If you have an isolated 30-day late payment, the FICO 8 score is more forgiving than the previous formula.

Maintaining good credit can save you a lot of money. Not just in a home mortgage (which could be a big number), but also in buying a car, furniture, or any other big-ticket item.

Figure 2.3: Credit Score Statistics[4]

In an effort to better understand your overall credit score, it is useful for you to see how your credit score matches up with the credit scores of others. This chart is designed to provide you an overview of such information to better aid you in developing a complete understanding of your credit score.

Score	Population	Rate of Delinquency
300–499	1%	87%
500–549	5%	71%
550–599	7%	51%
600–649	11%	31%
650–699	16%	15%
700–749	20%	5%
749–799	29%	2%
800 and up	11%	1%

4 Reprinted with permission of www.myFICO.com

Figure 2.4: Improving Your FICO® Credit Score [5]

It's important to note that raising your FICO credit score is a bit like losing weight. It takes time and there is no quick fix. In fact, quick fix efforts can backfire. The best advice is to manage credit responsibly over time. See how much money you can save by just following these tips and raising your credit score.

Payment History Tips:

- **Pay your bills on time.**
  Delinquent payments and collections can have a major negative impact on your FICO score.

- **If you have missed payments, get current and stay current.**
  The longer you pay your bills on time, the better your credit score

- **Be aware that paying off a collection account will not remove it from your credit report.**
  It will stay on your report for seven years.

- **If you are having trouble making ends meet, contact your creditors or see a legitimate credit counselor.**
  This won't improve your credit score immediately, but if you can begin to manage your credit and pay on time, your score will get better over time.

Amounts Owed Tips:

- **Keep balances low on credit cards and other "revolving credit."**
  High outstanding debt can affect a credit score .

- **Pay off debt rather than moving it around.**
  The most effective way to improve your credit score in this area is by paying down your revolving credit. In fact, owing the same amount but having fewer open accounts may lower your score.

---

5 Reprinted with permission of www.myFICO.com.

Figure 2.4: Improving Your FICO® Credit Score (Continued)

- **Don't close unused credit cards as a short-term strategy to raise your score.**

- **Don't open a number of new credit cards that you don't need, just to increase your available credit.**
  This approach could backfire and actually lower your credit score

Length of Credit History Tips:

- **If you have been managing credit for a short time, don't open a lot of new accounts too rapidly.**
  New accounts will lower your average account age, which will have a larger effect on your score if you don't have a lot of other credit information. Also, rapid account buildup can look risky if you are a new credit user.

New Credit Tips:

- **Re-establish your credit history if you have had problems.**
  Opening new accounts responsibly and paying them off on time will raise your credit score in the long term.

- **Note that it's OK to request and check your own credit report.**
  This won't affect your score, as long as you order your credit report directly from the credit reporting agency or through an organization authorized to provide credit reports to consumers

Types of Credit Use Tips:

- **Apply for and open new credit accounts only as needed.**
  Don't open accounts just to have a better credit mix—it probably won't raise your credit score.

- **Have credit cards, but manage them responsibly.**
  In general, having credit cards and installment loans (and paying timely payments) will raise your credit score. Someone with no credit cards, for example, tends to be higher risk than someone who has managed credit cards responsibly.

Figure 2.4: Improving Your FICO® Credit Score (Continued)

> • **Note that closing an account doesn't make it go away.**
>
> A closed account will still show up on your credit report, and may be considered in the score.

Myth # 19: If You Plan to Buy a Car and a House, It's Best to Buy the Car First

Fiction: If you just read Myth # 18, you know that buying anything on credit, including a car, will generally lower your credit score. If you want to purchase things like furniture or a car, and are buying a house, wait until the sale of the house closes before you put anything on credit.

Our agent, Carol, helped a very nice couple, Bill and Frieda, locate a house they wanted, and wrote an offer for them. Bill was just getting started as an accountant, and they were first-time home buyers. After two counter-offers, they agreed on a price and opened escrow. (This is an escrow state.) They had been pre-approved for a loan, so they initiated the loan process. The lender estimated that the loan would take 45 days, which was fine because they had 60 days to close.

The loan process ended up taking 10 days longer than anticipated, but they were still all right because they had 5 days left to close. That's when the trouble started. When the lender told Bill and Frieda that their loan was approved, they signed the loan documents right away. He told them that the loan would fund in 48 hours, and the sale would record the day after that, which was the 60th day. The next day Bill and Frieda went shopping and bought new furniture, a refrigerator, and a new car (which they had been holding off doing because Carol had told them to). Thinking that they were now safe, they bought all these items on credit, since they had used all their cash for the down payment and closing costs.

Carol then received a call from escrow saying the loan funding had been cancelled. After further inquiry, she found out that the lender had run a last-minute credit check, which showed all the new entries for their purchases. Because of the drop in their credit score and the new debt they had incurred,

Bill and Frieda no longer qualified for the loan to buy their house. Needless to say, they were devastated.

They did, however, have a new car and some furniture.

Myth # 20: I Need to Have a 20 Percent Down Payment to Buy a House

Fiction: A down payment for a house can be as little as 3.5 percent of the home's cost. The amount of your down payment depends on your credit score, your income, the cost of the home, and the type of mortgage. Generally, though, if your down payment is less than 20 percent, you will have to buy Private Mortgage Insurance (PMI).This protects the lender in case you default on the loan, which is more likely with a low down payment. The PMI premium varies, depending on the loan amount and other factors, and usually increases your interest rate by about 0.8 percent, which amounts to about $125 per month on a $250,000 loan.

Terminating PMI

Under the Homeowners Protection Act (HPA) of 1998, you have the right to request cancellation of PMI when you pay the loan down to 80 percent of the original purchase price. You must also have a good payment record with no 30-day late payments over the last 12 months, and no 60-day late payments in the last 24 months. In addition, under HPA, the lender must automatically cancel PMI when the homeowner's mortgage is paid down to 78 percent of the purchase price. (Some lenders may allow for appreciation in this calculation—dare to dream.) In addition, the lender must cancel PMI when the loan reaches the mid-point of its term, which would be 15 years for a 30-year loan.

The 3.5 percent down loan is a Federal Housing Authority (FHA) loan. This is covered in detail by Myth # 25. Also, for a veteran, there are circumstances where he can buy a house with nothing down. Such is the Veteran's Administration (VA) loan made by a mortgage broker and guaranteed by the Veteran's Administration itself.

Myth # 21: Loans are Difficult to Get for Almost Everyone

Fact: Since the financial meltdown in 2009, the mortgage lending industry has become ultra-conservative, to put it mildly. The industry is now very much in the public eye, with the federal government looking over its shoulder. In fact, Congress passed a financial overhaul bill in July 2010, which the President signed into law. The bill has made obtaining a home loan extremely difficult for anyone except those with stellar credit, and even they are being put through hoops.

Here is a brief overview of the loan process. It starts with a Uniform Residential Loan application. Once you have completed that, the lender will ask for information about your down payment and your income, including:

1. Pay stubs
2. W-2s
3. Bank statements
4. Tax returns
5. Expenses/payments

The lender will order an appraisal while he is verifying your income and expense information. He will also order a credit report. All this information is needed to qualify you for the loan. The approval cycle will take from 30 to 60 days, depending on the complexity of the borrower's situation. The average is 45 days. When the loan is approved the lender will order loan documents, which takes 24 to 48 hours. After you sign the loan documents, the lender will fund the loan, usually 24 hours later.

 TIP: If You are Obtaining a Loan to Buy a House, Make Sure You Have at Least 60 Days to Close.

Myth # 22: Applying to Multiple Lenders Will Damage Your Credit Score

Fiction: According to www.myFICO.com, if you are applying for a home mortgage, the FICO score will allow for rate shopping over a 30-day period.

Therefore, if you apply to several lenders during that period, it will only count as one inquiry.[6]

TIP: If You Apply to Multiple Lenders, Make Sure to Select One Within 30 Days of Your First Inquiry.

Myth # 23: I Should Find a House to Buy First, Then Apply for a Loan

Fiction: If you find a house you can't live without before being pre-approved by your lender, you are doomed to disappointment. If you make an offer, the seller won't accept it. He will not wait until you are pre-approved. As for having a pre-qualification letter, our view is that it is a worthless piece of paper.

Besides, you may not even qualify to buy the house.

How would you know?

Myth # 24: You Can Increase Your Credit Score by Making More Money

Fiction: According to www.myFICO.com, this is not true. The following factors are not considered in your FICO score.[7]

1. Your race, color, religion, national origin, sex, or marital status

2. Your age

3. Your salary or occupation

4. Where you live

Myth # 25: I Can't Qualify for an FHA Loan

Fiction: The FHA loan has many features that make it desirable:

1. It is easier to qualify for because it is an insured loan

2. You don't need perfect credit; with a credit score of 580, you can qualify for a low down payment loan.

6 Reprinted with permission of www.myFICO.com
7 ibid.

3. You can buy with a low down payment: only 3.5 percent down, and that can come from family members.[8]

Also, the loan limit in high-cost areas is $729,750, which widens the prospects. These loans do require Mortgage Insurance Premium (MIP). Similar to the PMI, it added 0.55 percent to the interest rate, and an up-front fee of 2.25 percent of the loan amount.

In August 2010, FHA Commissioner David H. Stevens announced a new Mortgage Insurance Premium (MIP) structure, which took effect on all new loans originated after October 4, 2010. The new structure consists of the following:

1. The up-front fee will be reduced from the current 2.25 percent to 1.00 percent.

2. The monthly premium will go up from the current 0.55 percent to 0.85 percent for loans up to 95 percent of loan-to-value, and to 0.90 percent for loans above 95 percent.

3. Sellers' concessions will be reduced from the current maximum of 6 percent to a maximum of 3 percent of the sales price.

4. The minimum FICO score to obtain an FHA loan will be 500. For a score between 500 and 579, the borrower will have to put 10 percent down. At 580 and above, the down payment will be 3.5 percent.

On February 14, 2011, FHA announced yet another change in MIP premiums, all monthly rates will increase by 0.25% on loans originated after April 17, 2011. This means a new monthly rate of 1.10 % on loans up to 95% and 1.15% for over 95%. The upfront fee will remain unchanged at 1.00%.

Fred and June were a young couple looking for their first house. They didn't have much in the way of savings, but really wanted their own place. They called on an ad in the paper, and went into the real estate office to meet with the listing agent. She showed them the house, and they liked it. Back at the office, the agent started writing an offer. She asked Fred and June

---

8   U.S. Department of Housing and Urban Development

how much of their savings they wanted to use for a down payment. She was horrified at their response. They told her that they had $10,000. She said they would need $40,000, and that there was no possibility they could buy a home with $10,000.

Fred and June left the office, dejected. The next day, Fred went to his office and told a friend about his problem. The friend suggested that Fred talk to the Human Resources department, perhaps they could help. The woman in HR told Fred that they were using an agent at our office for relocating their personnel, and suggested that he call to see if she had any ideas. Fred called our agent, Beverly, and they met with her. Upon hearing that they only had $10,000, Beverly told them about FHA financing, which required a small 3.5 percent down payment.

Fred and June felt renewed hope, and Beverly referred them to an FHA lender who pre-approved them for a loan of $220,000. Beverly then showed them several homes in their price range. They found one they liked that was priced at $210,000 and made a full- price offer. To their joy, the offer was accepted by the seller. They immediately started the loan process and closed the sale 60 days later.

Beverly had turned their dream into a reality.

Myth # 26: When Getting a Loan, It is Best to Work Directly with a Bank

Fiction: There is nothing wrong with working with a bank. If you have a good relationship with your bank, use it. But banks are generally limited to their own loan products. When you work with a mortgage broker, they have access to a wide variety of loan products not available to an individual bank, plus they usually can sell the bank's products as well. Just make sure that you get a good, reliable mortgage broker by obtaining a referral, as discussed in Myth # 22.

(Note: To obtain a FREE report "Finding the Best Mortgage," go to page 211.)

Section 3:
<u>ADVENTURES IN SHORT SALES</u>

Having to go through a foreclosure or a bankruptcy is not fun. Either one will destroy your credit and your self-esteem. However, there is an alternative called a "short sale." This section will explain what a short sale is, and how it affects buyers and sellers. It will give you tips on how best to handle a short sale, and how to steer clear of trouble.

Myth # 27: Tall People Can't Utilize a Short Sale

Fiction: Tall people have their own set of problems, but this is not one of them. They are not discriminated against when it comes to short sales, along with medium-size people and short people. If you want to find out who does qualify, read on.

Myth # 28: Short Sales are Simple and Easy

Fiction: A short sale is a transaction in which the lender agrees to allow the borrower to sell his property "short" of the balance owed on the loan. Hence, the term "short sale." In this situation, the owner's mortgage balance is greater than the probable sales price of the home. Since the lender has not yet foreclosed, this creates a window of opportunity for the owner to sell the property on his own.

It is, however, a complicated process. The biggest problem in a short sale is that the homeowner must persuade his lender to discount the loan.

It becomes even more complicated when there is a second mortgage and/or an equity line. These lenders must also agree to discount their loans.

Not an easy task, as you might imagine.

The process starts when the homeowner receives an acceptable offer. He must then submit a "Short Sale Package" to each of the lenders. This package consists of numerous components, as outlined in Figure 3.1, and is typical of what Realtors submit to lenders. If any element is missing or incomplete, the process will be delayed. The key ingredient is the seller's hardship letter. A sample seller's hardship letter is shown in Figure 3.2.

The large increase in number of short sales has created a new job title:

Short Sale Negotiator. This is an individual who will, for a fee, negotiate with your bank to obtain a reduction in the amount of their loan. He must, however, have a real estate license and work for a broker.

Once the lender agrees to a short sale, they will issue an "Approval Letter" stating the terms they find acceptable. An example of a lender's approval letter is shown in Figure 3.3.

You might ask why lenders would ever agree to discount a loan. There are many reasons, but the primary consideration is that they will lose less money than by going through the lengthy foreclosure process.

Once the lender's approval letter is received, you can open escrow (if you are in an escrow state) and proceed with the transaction in the usual manner. If you are in a state that doesn't use escrow, you proceed with the transaction in the usual manner.

TIP: Make Sure Your Agent is Trained and Certified in Handling Short Sales

Figure 3.1: Components of a Short Sale Package[9]

1. Cover Letter, containing an overview of the homeowner's situation

2. Short Sale Application Form

3. Letter of Authorization. This allows the seller's agent to deal directly with the lender.

4. Sellers Financial Information, with supporting documentation

   a. Financial Statement of assets and liabilities

   b. Two years of tax returns

   c. Three months of bank statements

   d. Pay stubs for the last two paydays

   e. List of monthly expenses

   f. Profit and Loss Statement, if self-employed

5. Seller's Hardship Information, with supporting documentation

   a. Medical bills

   b. Divorce decree

   c. Disability statements

   d. Unemployment status

   e. HOA liens

6. Comparative Market Analysis (CMA)

   a. Using the most recent comparables to establish market value

7. Signed Purchase Agreement

8. Written proof of the buyer's ability to purchase the property

9. Copy of certified escrow instructions, if applicable

10. Sellers Net Proceeds Sheet

11. Preliminary Title Report

---

9 Reprinted with permission of the Real Estate Buyer's Agent Council (REBAC), a wholly owned subsidiary of the National Association of Realtors. Copyright 2009, REBAC

Figure 3.2: Sample Seller's Hardship Letter[10]

To Whom It May Concern:

This is a very difficult thing to write. I have always been able to pay my debts in the past and am truly sorry that I cannot do so now.

I lost my job as a manager for a large home improvement company. I have been unemployed for six months. I have been receiving unemployment benefits. However, my unemployment check replaces about one-quarter of my previous income. My wife is a stay-at-home mom responsible for our four children. We have both been looking for employment. We have exhausted our savings. Our credit cards are maxed out and we are in the processing of filing for divorce.

We can no longer afford to make the $1,800 monthly mortgage payments on our home. We are currently five months behind and see no way to make up the $9,000 in back payments. Our real estate taxes are also due and we have no way to pay those either.

We have agreed to sell our property for $375,000. It has been on the market for over 60 days and this is the only offer we have received. We want to avoid a foreclosure sale that will further damage our credit. We respectfully request that you consider this offer and work with our agent to negotiate a short-sale transaction.

We have exhausted all of our options and the only next step is letting the property go to foreclosure.

Sincerely,

Daniel and Sandy Smith

---

10   Reprinted with permission of the Real Estate Buyer's Agent Council (REBAC), a wholly owned subsidiary of the National Association of Realtors. Copyright 2009 REBAC

Figure 3.3: Sample Lender Approval Letter[11]

Date: May 7, 2009

Dear Borrower:

In response to your request for a sale of the above-referenced property for less than the total payoff of the property, Joes' Servicing Company (JSC) hereby agrees to the short sale between Sam and Sally Smith, the seller(s) and Bob and Betty Brown, the buyer(s) and will release its lien contingent upon the following terms:

1. With a purchase of $300,000 in which the required minimum net proceeds for JSC loan number 12367893 should be no less than $262,404.51. The settlement/closing is scheduled on or before 6/7/09.

2. Any extension of the closing date requires the written approval of Joe's Servicing Company.

3. A copy of the HUD1 Settlement Statement (preliminary) must be faxed to JSC. This fax should be sent to 555-555-5555 or e-mailed to joe@jsc.com. Do not close without an approved HUD from JSC.

4. IN NO EVENT SHALL THE BORROWER RECEIVE ANY FUNDS FROM THE SALE OF THIS PROPERTY. Any surplus funds above the agreed-upon Short Sale purchase price at the time of closing is the exclusive property of JSC and shall be made payable to JSC. The mortgagor(s) also waive their rights to any escrowed funds or refunds from prepaid expenses.

5. The following items are in agreement to be paid at closing:

   1. Second lien to receive $5,000

   2. Commission paid to be no more than $8,000

   3. Closing costs paid to be $37,595.49

   4. Any outstanding settlement costs to be paid by Seller(s), Buyer(s) or Agent

Upon satisfaction of all terms of this approval, the mortgage will be discharged and a release document will be forwarded for recording. If a foreclosing action was commenced against the property, then upon satisfaction of all terms of this approval, the pending foreclosure action will be dismissed and appropriate instruments recorded.

A client we will call Mary came to us for help with a short sale. Mary had been widowed two years earlier and could no longer afford her house payments. She had previously listed her house with her niece, Sarah, who had just received her real estate license, but worked full time as a receptionist at a dental office.

After receiving an offer, Sarah requested a short sale approval from the lender, who sent back a list if items required for approval. (Apparently, Sarah hadn't been trained in how to handle a short sale.) To shorten a short sale story, by the time Sarah sent the information to the bank, the buyer already left to purchase a different house. After this happened three more times, Mary gave up and came to us for help. We assigned her to a trained short-sale agent, and Mary's house sold without incident.

There is a recent development in short sales. On November 30, 2009, the U.S. Department of the Treasury released guidelines for its Home Affordable Foreclosure Alternatives Program (HAFA), which took effect on April 5, 2010, and will be effective through December 31, 2012. To be eligible for the program, you must meet the following criteria:[12]

1. Property must be a principal residence.

2. First lien must have originated prior to January 1, 2009.

3. Loan must be in default, or default must be imminent.

4. Total pay-off cannot exceed $729,750.

5. Monthly payment must exceed 31 percent of homeowner's gross income. (Note: This requirement was deleted by a 12/28/2010 Supplemental Directive, effective 2/1/ 2011.)

6. Borrower does not qualify for a loan modification under the HAMP Program. (See Myth # 45.)

---

12   U.S. Department of the Treasury

The program provides alternatives to foreclosure with a short sale or a Deed-in-Lieu of foreclosure. For short sales, the lender will provide you with a list price and the terms of sale that are acceptable to him. This includes his net proceeds and acceptable sales costs. That way, you will know what the lender will accept before listing your house. Then you can list your house with a local realtor at the approved price.

When you receive an offer, you submit it along with the required short-sale documentation to the lender.

If the offer meets all his requirements, the lender will approve it, and you can proceed to close the transaction.

The HAFA program also provides financial incentives. The homeowner receives $3,000 for relocation assistance, the loan servicer receives $1,500 for processing costs, and the investor receives up to $2,000 for his subordinate position.[13]

The HAFA timelines are documented in Figure 3.4.

A HAFA Deed-in-Lieu may be offered by the lender if the home doesn't sell within the approved marketing period. In this case, the lender accepts title to the property in exchange for cancelling the mortgage.

 TIP: The Seller Should Make Sure That He Gets a Release for the Note as Well as the Deed of Trust as Part of the Settlement.

Be Aware of Short Sale Fraud

You need to be aware of the types of fraud prevalent in short sale transactions:

1. **Short sale flipping** – unlicensed "facilitators" convince banks to accept very low offers based on questionable appraisals, and resell the property at a higher price before it closes.

2. **Payments outside of the transaction** – payments are made to third parties, like a short sale facilitator, without disclosure to the lender or reporting it on the HUD-1 statement. There are many variations of this.

---

13 Freddie Mac, used with permission

These practices are in violation of federal law. Don't get involved in them

Figure 3.4: HAFA Timelines[14]
(Modified by a 12/28/2010 Supplemental Directive, effective 2/1/2011.)

1. The loan servicer must notify the homeowner that a short sale is an option with a written Short Sale Agreement (SSA). This agreement will include:

   - Net proceeds acceptable to the lender.

   - An agreement not to complete a foreclosure sale if the borrower complies with the SSA terms.

   - Amount of closing costs acceptable to the lender.

   - Notice that the sale must be an arms-length transaction.

   - Notice that buyer agrees not to resell the property for at least 90 days after closing.

   - An agreement to fully release the borrower from any liability for repayment of the loan.

2. The homeowner then has 14 days to respond to the SSA.

3. After the SSA is signed and returned to the lender, the homeowner has 120 days to sell to property.

4. Within 3 business days of receiving a signed Purchase Agreement, the homeowner must submit a completed "Request for Approval of Short Sale" (RASS) to the loan servicer, along with

   - A copy of the Purchase Agreement and all addendums.

   - Documentation of buyer's funds and a commitment letter from his lender.

   - Status of subordinate liens.

---

14 Freddie Mac, used with permission

Figure 3.4: HAFA Timelines (continued)

5. Within 30 calendar days after the loan servicer has received the RASS, he must approve or deny the request, and notify the homeowner.

6. The servicer may specify the closing date, but no sooner than 45 days after the date of the Purchase Agreement.

7. The loan servicer must release the first mortgage lien within 10 business days after receiving the proceeds of the short sale.

Myth # 29: Short Sales Can be Done Rather Quickly

Fiction: Short sales are not short. The average time for a lender to review to review and approve a short sale is about three months, with another month to close. If your house is in foreclosure and you want to pursue a short sale, you can see the need for urgency.

Note: If the homeowner uses the Home Affordable Foreclosure Alternatives (HAFA) Program (See Myth # 28), the timeframe will be shorter.

Melinda was a young, very talented interior designer. A couple of years earlier, she had purchased a house with her boyfriend, Bob. He was an engineer, but decided that he wanted to go into business for himself, so he quit his job. They then took out a $90,000 second mortgage on the home to finance the business. The business required sales skills, which Bob lacked, so immediately the business started losing money. To make matters worse, in their attempt to keep the business alive, they took out a third mortgage of $50,000, a hard-money loan at a very high rate of interest.

Finally, they ran out of money, and had to close the business. Bob contacted our agent, Jane, to help them sell the house. She inspected the property and told them that they needed to make some repairs to get it in market condition. She suggested a contractor who could do the work and bill escrow, so they didn't have to put out any money. Jane also told them that the market was starting to turn, and that they had better make the repairs quickly, before the market went further down.

Being an engineer and out of work, Bob decided that he would do the repairs himself. Three months later, he still wasn't finished, so Jane insisted that they put the house on the market anyway. By this time, between the three mortgages, they owed about $750,000, so Jane listed the property at $835,000. They received an offer for $795,000, which would have paid their mortgages and costs, but Bob refused to sell at that price. After a heated argument with Melinda, Bob decided to move out and file for bankruptcy. Melinda now had to deal with the problem on her own. By the time Jane had the house released from bankruptcy, it was another 30 days, and the market had dropped dramatically.

Melinda now had no choice but to try a short sale. Fortunately, Jane was skilled in short sales. After reducing the price to $650,000, they received an offer for $600,000. Jane submitted a short sale package to the lender, but by the time they got back to her, they had lost the buyer. The house finally sold to another buyer, and closed for $550,000. As part of the settlement, Melinda had to sign a note to repay $30,000 of the forgiven debt. Of course Bob had no liability because of the bankruptcy.

If your house is in foreclosure, you need sufficient time to accomplish a short sale before the foreclosure is completed. So time is of the essence if you want to go the short sale route.

 TIP: If You Have a Valid Purchase Contract with a Qualified Buyer, the Lender will Often Postpone the Foreclosure Sale to allow Sufficient Time to Close.

Myth # 30: Any Homeowner Can Do a Short Sale

Fiction: In order to qualify for a short sale, you must have a valid hardship.[15]

Loss of equity is not considered a hardship. Eligible hardships are:

- Loss of job
- Business failure
- Illness or medical bills

---

15   Reprinted with permission of the Real Estate Buyer's Agent Council (REBAC), a wholly owned subsidiary of the National Association of Realtors. Copyright 2009, REBAC

- Divorce or death of spouse
- Natural disaster

Rebecca was a single mom and a psychology teacher. She decided to go back to school and obtain her master's degree, so she refinanced her home and quit her job. For two years she lived on the cash from the refinance while she pursued her degree.

After obtaining her degree, she went back to work, only to be laid off a month later because of budget cuts. By this time, the economy had deteriorated, and the housing market was a disaster, especially on the high end. She had run out of money and could no longer make her house payments. To further complicate matters, the bank filed a notice of foreclosure. Rebecca was referred to our agent, Christine, who assessed the situation and suggested that Rebecca contact an attorney for advice. The attorney said that a short sale would be her best option. She now owed over $1 million on the property, which had a current market value of about $600,000. Christine put the house on the market for $650,000 and received several offers right away.

She submitted a Short Sale Package to the bank, and contacted the bank's loss mitigation department to find out which negotiator had been assigned to this property. After 30 days, the negotiator no longer responded to her e-mails, so Christine contacted a loss-mitigation supervisor. The supervisor informed her that a new negotiator had been assigned, and he would have to re-evaluate the package. The negotiator was then replaced two more times.

This process had consumed 90 days, and the bank had now scheduled the property for a trustee sale. Christine had to request that the current negotiator obtain a postponement of the trustee sale, which was happening in two weeks. After another 10 days, the negotiator approved the highest offer, which was $575,000. It finally closed 30 days later.

Myth # 31: A Short Sale Has No Advantage over a Foreclosure

Fiction: A short sale has many advantages over a foreclosure. Some of them are:

1. It won't damage your credit score as much as a foreclosure

2. You can qualify for a mortgage sooner

3. It will have a lesser impact on nearby home values

In addition, you won't have to go through the painful, unsettling foreclosure process.

Myth # 32: You Have to be Behind in Your Payments to Qualify for a Short Sale

Fiction: Unless you are using the HAFA program, you do not have to be behind in your payments to qualify. You must be considered a hardship case to qualify and owe more than the current market value of the home.

However, if you apply to the HAFA program, you must be delinquent, or close to it, to qualify for a short sale.

Myth # 33: You Have to Pay Federal Income Tax on Short Sale Forgiven Debt

Fiction: Under the Mortgage Forgiveness Act of 2007, a homeowner will not be taxed on cancellation of debt provided the following conditions are met:

1. Property is the taxpayer's principal residence.

2. Cancelled debt is Qualified Principal Residence Indebtedness, which is a loan used to acquire or build a principal residence. The maximum debt cannot exceed $1 million for married people filing separately, or $2 million for joint returns.[16]

The act was effective for calendar years 2007 through 2009. However, the Emergency Economic Stabilization Act of 2008 extended the program through December 31, 2012.

16 Freddie Mac, used with permission.

There are other circumstances where the homeowner is exempt from federal income tax on the forgiven debt: when the taxpayer is insolvent, or the debt is discharged in bankruptcy.

Note: Some states may require payment of state income tax on the forgiven debt.

In all other cases, as with investment property, the amount of the forgiven debt is considered income to the taxpayer, and is subject to federal income tax. The IRS requires the lender to issue a Form 1099 for the amount of the forgiven debt.

Myth # 34: If You Fall Back on a Short Sale, the Lender Can Collect the Deficiency from You

Fiction: Under HAFA, the borrower is fully released from any liability from all participating lenders. That means no promissory notes or deficiency judgments. Prior to closing, the first lien holder is required to obtain written agreement from all subordinate lenders that they will release the borrower from any further liability, provided that they receive the agreed-upon funds.[17]

If you are not in the HAFA program, the lender could require you to sign a promissory note for all or part of the deficiency as a condition of doing a short sale. If you default on a promissory note, the lender can obtain a deficiency judgment against you and attach assets such as your bank account or your salary.

Some states, like California, have a non-recourse mortgage law. After foreclosing on a purchase money loan, the lender cannot look to the borrower to pay the deficiency.

> *TIP: If You are in a Non-Recourse Mortgage State and Don't Have the Resources to Pay a Promissory Note, Look into Foreclosure as an Option. On a Purchase Money Loan, the Lender Cannot Obtain a Deficiency Judgment against You. Check with your Attorney.*

---

17 Freddie Mac, used with permission

Myth # 35: A Short Sale Doesn't Affect Your Credit

Fiction: According to www.myFICO.com, our clients and other sources, a homeowner with previously good credit could see his credit score drop 100 or more points. It depends upon how the short sale is reported to the credit bureaus. If the lender reports the short sale as being settled for less than the full balance, it will stay on the homeowner's credit report for seven years.

Myth # 36: After a Short Sale, You Endure a Long Wait Before You Can Buy Another House.

Fact: Freddie Mac may allow you to buy another house after two years. The wait for an FHA loan is three years.[18]

 TIP: Always Obtain Legal and Tax Advice before Deciding between a Short Sale and a Foreclosure.

---

18 Freddie Mac, used with permission

Section 4:
SPOTLIGHT ON FORECLOSURES

Foreclosure is a legal process by which the lender takes back ownership of a property from a defaulted buyer. This process is different in every state and, in different locales, can take anywhere from 32 days to a year. The norm is about 120 days. A typical foreclosure timeline (representing California law) is illustrated in Figure 4.1.

According to real estate economists, the number of bank-owned properties is expected to increase through 2012, and then gradually decline over the next three to five years. Clearly, foreclosures are going to be with us for a very long time.

This section will cover the details of foreclosures, and how they affect homeowners. It will give you tips on how to avoid foreclosure and foreclosure scams, the best time to buy in the foreclosure cycle, and how to minimize problems.

Myth # 37: You Can Make Money by Buying a Bank Repossession (REO)

Fiction: An REO (Real Estate Owned) property is one that goes back to the lender after an unsuccessful foreclosure auction. (See Myth # 46.) The bank now owns the property, and the loan no longer exists. The bank will normally evict any occupants and may or may not make some repairs.

An REO is typically not a great bargain because the lender has incurred significant costs in foreclosing and is looking to recover those costs. In addition, you may have to make substantial repairs to put the property in marketable condition.

TIP: Do Your Homework Before Buying an REO.

Figure 4.1: Foreclosure Action Timeline[19] (California)

Day 1	----------------------	Record Notice of Default
Within 10 day	----------------------	Mail Notice of Default Public Notice of Default when Necessary
Within 1 month	----------------------	Mail Notice of Default
After 3 months	----------------------	Set Sale Date
25 days before sale date	----------------------	Send Notice of Sale to IRS—when Necessary, IRS Regulations
20 days before sale date	----------------------	Public Notice of Sale Post Notice of Sale Mail Notice of Sale, California
Within 10 days from first publication notice of sale	----------------------	Request for directions to property sent to beneficiary
14 days before sale date	----------------------	Request Notice of Sale
7 days before sale date	----------------------	Trustee cannot sell for 7 days after expiration of court orders
5 business days before sale date	----------------------	Right to reinstate
Sale date	----------------------	Sold!

---

19 Reprinted with permission of Pickford Escrow

Harry and Pam were experienced buyers, having moved several times. They were introduced to our agent, Sharon, to help them buy a house. They were well qualified and were looking in the $500,000 to $600,000 price range. They had also heard that you could save a lot of money by buying a bank-owned property, so they asked Sharon to find one for them.

After looking at several homes, they found one they wanted to buy. The bank had just taken the property back and had made no repairs. That suited Harry; he figured they could get a better price that way. The house was in pretty rough condition, but it was in a good neighborhood. It was listed at $610,000, so they offered $550,000. After several counter-offers, they accepted a price of $580,000.

After conducting a property inspection, they found that the home needed new flooring, window coverings, all new appliances, and a paint job, both inside and out. Harry figured that they were still all right because they were $30,000 below the asking price.

Once they closed the sale, they started getting estimates for all the repairs. As it turned out, the carpet cost $4,500, drapes $5,400, appliances $5,200, painting $3,900, repair of cabinets and other items $6,500, and replacing baseboards $2,800, for a grand total of $36,300. Harry and Pam had now invested $616,300.

They could have purchased a similar house needing no work for $610,000.

Myth # 38: Foreclosed Homes are Found Only in Bad Neighborhoods

Fiction: Foreclosed properties are appearing more frequently in upscale neighborhoods. There was a recent bank-owned property for sale in our area for $12.9 million. It was previously owned by a Hollywood personality.

Apparently, no one is immune from the recession.

Myth # 39:   When Buying a House during the Foreclosure Process, it is Best to Buy in the Pre-Foreclosure Position

Fact: Pre-foreclosure is the period between when the notice of default is filed and the property is sold at auction. Myth # 37 explained why you may not want to buy a property after the bank has taken it back. Therefore, if you absolutely must have a foreclosure, this is the best time to buy. The benefit here is that you are dealing directly with the homeowner, which is always the better choice. Depending upon his situation, the homeowner may be able to execute a short sale, which would be to your benefit.

Myth # 40: A Foreclosure Won't Adversely Affect Your Credit

Fiction: According to www.myFICO.com, our clients, and other sources, your credit score could drop up to 200 points after a foreclosure, and it will remain on your credit report for seven years.

Myth # 41: Foreclosed Homes Always Need a Lot of Work

Fiction: Some banks will completely rehab their REOs; others will just do cosmetic work, such as paint and carpeting. A few will do absolutely nothing.

It all depends on the lender.

Tony and Linda were working with our agent, Mike, to find a home. They were a young couple just getting started and had limited resources. Mike showed them a newer neighborhood in their price range that consisted mostly of younger people with small children. There wasn't much on the market, and nothing they saw appealed to them. About a week after their first outing, Mike called Tony and Linda with the news that a new listing just came on the market, but it was a bank-owned property.

Tony and Linda were skeptical because they had heard that bank-owned properties were usually pretty rough, and they had no extra money to handle repairs. They figured, however, that it wouldn't hurt to look, so Mike took them to see the house.

When they opened the door, it was like an episode from *Extreme Makeover, Home Edition*. Linda shrieked and started crying. Tony kept saying, "Oh my gosh, Oh my gosh." The bank had completely rehabbed the house! It had new carpeting, new entry tile, new kitchen cabinets, countertops, flooring, and all the built-in appliances had been replaced.

The house had been repainted, inside and out. It looked like a brand-new home. Tony and Linda could move right in without spending a dime. They immediately made a full-price offer of $385,000, which the bank accepted. Forty-five days later, they moved in, still amazed at their good fortune—and thankful for Mike.

Myth # 42: Foreclosures Don't Affect your Ability to Buy Another Home

Fiction: According to Freddie Mac, the wait to buy another home is five years after the completed foreclosure sale. If you were an investor, or didn't live in the home, the wait is seven years. To make a loan after a foreclosure, lenders are looking for re-established credit with a FICO score of at least 680.

Myth # 43: A Homeowner Has a Redemption Period after a Foreclosure Sale Where He Can Regain Title to His Home

Fact: Sometimes true, sometimes not. The redemption period varies from state to state. Some states have no redemption period, others allow up to a year. Most require you to pay all past-due payments, plus costs, to redeem your home.

This is another reason to be careful if you are going to buy an REO.

Myth # 44: I Can Stay in My House for 30 Days after the Bank Has Repossessed It.

Fiction: You are no longer a legal resident of your house after the bank has taken ownership. In most states, the lender can evict you immediately. This applies to tenants, also; their lease becomes null and void after foreclosure.

 TIP: Contact Your Lender before They Have Taken Ownership and Find out What Their Eviction Policy Is. You Might Be Able to Stay Longer.

Myth # 45: When You Can't Make Your House Payments, It Is Nearly Impossible to Avoid Foreclosure

Fiction: There are many options to pursue before you got to foreclosure.[20]

1. **Home Affordable Refinance Program (HARP)** – Offers a new loan with lower interest rates and payments. (See Figure 4.2)

2. **Repayment Plan** – You can repay past-due amounts in a payment plan over time, in addition to your regular payment.

3. **Forbearance** – the lender reduces or suspends mortgage payments temporarily. The amount is usually added on to the end of the loan.

4. **Loan Modification (HAMP)** – reduces interest rate and payments. (See Figure 4.3)

5. **Short Sale** – You sell your home for less than the mortgage balance, and the lender takes a discount. Use the Home Affordable Foreclosure Alternatives Program (HAFA), if possible. (See Myth # 28)

6. **Deed-in-Lieu of Foreclosure** – The lender accepts transfer of title in exchange for cancelling the mortgage debt.(See Myth # 28)

Some additional tips to avoid foreclosure are provided in Figure 4.4.

In August 2010, the U. S. Treasury Department announced that it would provide $2 billion to 17 states that have unemployment rates higher than the national average, in order to aid the unemployed and help them save their homes from foreclosure. The program, called the Housing Finance Agency Innovation Fund for the Hardest Hit Housing Markets (HHF), will provide funding to the eligible states Housing Finance Agency (HFA), from the federal Housing Finance Agency.

Another $1 billion will go to the U.S. Department of Housing and Urban Development (HUD) for a new program that will provide homeowners with emergency loans of up to $50,000, with no interest or payments for up to two years.

There really are a lot of options. Take advantage of them.

---

20 U.S. Department of the Treasury

Figure 4.2: Home Affordable Refinance Program (HARP)[21]

To be eligible, you must meet the following requirements:

1. You must be the owner-occupant of your home.
2. Your loan must be guaranteed by Fannie Mae or Freddie Mac
3. You must be current on your mortgage payment.
4. Your loan cannot exceed 125 percent of your home's market value
5. You must have the ability to make the new payment

HARP's objective is to provide homeowners who have good credit an opportunity to reduce their payments with a new loan. The program expires on June 10, 2011. To find out if you have a Fannie Mae or Freddie Mac loan, ask your lender or call:

1-800-7 FANNIE for Fannie Mae, or

1- 800- FREDDIE for Freddie Mac

8 a.m. to 8 p.m., Eastern Standard Time

21 U.S. Department of the Treasury

Figure 4.3: Home Affordable Modification Program (HAMP)[22]

HAMP is designed to help homeowners struggling to avoid foreclosure by modifying their loan so that they can make their payments over the long term.

Eligibility requirements are:

1. Mortgage was originated prior to January 1, 2009
2. Principle loan balance less than $729,750.
3. Total monthly payment, including taxes and insurance, exceeds 31 percent of gross income
4. Home is occupied by the owner as a primary residence
5. Owner has a financial hardship and is delinquent on the mortgage

To reduce the owner's mortgage payment to less than 31 percent of his income, the lender will reduce the interest rate to as low as 2 percent and may extend the loan up to 40 years. The lender may also defer some of the principal until the end of the loan.

---

22   U.S. Department of Housing and Urban Development

Figure 4.4: Tips to Avoid Foreclosure[23]

1. **Don't Ignore the Problem**

   The further behind you become, the more likely you that will lose your home.

2. **Contact Your Lender Right Away**

   Lenders don't want your house, and they have options. Call them.

3. **Open and Respond to all Mail from Your Lender**

   This is very important. Missing deadlines could cause you to lose your home.

4. **Know Your Rights**

   Learn all about the foreclosure laws and time frames in your state.

5. **Understand Your Options**

   They are outlined in Myth # 45.

6. **Contact a HUD-Approved Housing Counselor**

   Call 1-800-569-4287 to find one near you.

7. **Prioritize Your Spending**

   After healthcare, make house payments your first priority.

8. **Use Your Assets**

   Sell whatever you can to pay your mortgage.

9. **Avoid Foreclosure-Prevention Companies**

   HUD will provide a free counselor; don't pay for help.

10. **Don't Lose Your Home to a Foreclosure-Recovery Scam**

    Review list of scams that follows.

---

23 U.S. Department of Housing and Urban Development

Avoid Foreclosure Scams.

Some of the more common scams are:[24]

1. **Lease-Back Scheme** – You are asked to transfer title to your home to the scammer who will, supposedly, obtain new financing, allow you to remain in the home as a renter, and eventually allow you to buy it back.

    All they want is your house and your money.

2. **Fake "Government" Modification Programs** – The scammer will claim to be affiliated with, or approved by, a government agency and require you to pay high up-front fees. You do not have to pay for legitimate government programs.

3. **Bankruptcy Scams** – The scammer will encourage you to file for bankruptcy, saying, "It's the only way …" Filing for bankruptcy is rarely, if ever, a permanent solution to prevent foreclosure. In addition, it will negatively impact your credit score and remain on your credit report for 10 years.

4. **Debt-Elimination Schemes** – The scammer will tell you to stop paying your mortgage, and they will be able to eliminate your debts.

    Don't stop making your payments.

5. **Foreclosure "Rescue" and Refinance Fraud** – The scam artist offers to act as an intermediary between you and the lender to negotiate a loan modification. He usually asks for a large up-front fee.

    Additional warning signs are shown in Figure 4.5.

---

24 U.S. Department of the Treasury

Figure 4.5: Ten Warning Signs of a Mortgage Modification Scam[25]

1. **"Pay us $1,000 and we'll save your home."**

   Some legitimate housing counselors may charge small fees, but fees that amount to thousands of dollars are likely a sign of potential fraud—especially if they are charged up -front, before the "counselor" has done any work for you. Be wary of companies that require you to provide a cashier's check or wire transfer before they take any action on your behalf.

2. **"I guarantee I will save your home—trust me."**

   Beware of guarantees that a person or company can stop foreclosure and allow you to remain in your house. Unrealistic promises are a sign that the person making them will not consider your particular circumstances and is unlikely to provide services that will actually help you.

3. **"Sign over your home, and we'll let you stay in it."**

   Be very suspicious if someone offers to pay your mortgage and rent your home back to you in exchange for transferring title to your home. Signing over the deed to another person gives that person the power to evict you, raise your rent, or sell the house. Although you will no longer own your home, you still will be legally responsible for paying the mortgage on it.

4. **"Stop paying your mortgage."**

   Do not trust anyone who tells you to stop making payments to your lender and servicer, even if that person says it will be done for you.

5. **"If your lender calls, don't talk to them."**

   Your lender should be your first point of contact for negotiating a repayment plan, modification, or short sale. It is vital to your interests to stay in close communication with your lender and servicer, so they understand your circumstances.

---

25 U.S. Department of the Treasury

Figure 4.5: Ten Warning Signs of a Mortgage Modification Scam (continued)

6. **"Your lender never had the legal authority to make a loan."**

   Do not listen to anyone who claims that "secret laws" or "secret information" will be used to eliminate your debt and have your mortgage contract declared invalid. These scammers use sham legal arguments to claim that you are not obligated to pay your mortgage. These arguments don't work.

7. **"Just sign this now; we'll fill in the blanks later."**

   Take the time to read and understand anything you sign. Never let anyone else fill out paperwork for you. Don't let anyone pressure you into signing anything that you don't agree with or understand.

8. **"Call 1-800-Fed-Loan."**

   This may be a scam. Some companies trick borrowers into believing that they are affiliated with or are approved by the government, or tell you that you must pay them high fees to qualify for government loan modification programs. Keep in mind that you do not have to pay to participate in legitimate government programs. All you need to do is contact your lender to find out if you qualify.

9. **"File for bankruptcy and keep your home."**

   Filing for bankruptcy only temporarily stops foreclosure. If your mortgage payments are not made, the bankruptcy court will eventually allow your lender to foreclose on your home. Be aware that some scammers will file bankruptcy in your name, without your knowledge, to temporarily stop foreclosure and make it seem as though they have negotiated a new payment agreement with your lender.

Figure 4.5: Ten Warning Signs of a Mortgage Modification Scam (continued)

> **10. "Why haven't you replied to our offer? Do you want to live on the streets?"**
>
> High-pressure tactics signal trouble. If someone continually contacts you and pressures you to work with them to stop foreclosure, do not work with that person. Legitimate housing counselors do not conduct business that way.

Protect Yourself from Scams

Below are a few ways to protect yourself from mortgage modification and foreclosure avoidance scams:[26]

- **Contact your lender first** – Call the loss mitigation department to find out your alternatives.

- **Make all mortgage payments directly to your lender** – Do not trust anyone to do it for you, and do not stop making payments.

- **Avoid paying up-front fees** – Do not pay fees to anyone before receiving services. Make sure you are dealing with a legitimate organization.

- **Know what you are signing** – Read and understand every document you sign. Do not rely on oral explanations. Never sign anything with blank spaces to be filled in later! If you don't understand it, have a lawyer review it.

- **Do not sign your deed without consulting an attorney** –– Scams often involve transfer of ownership of your home to a scammer. By signing over your deeds you lose all rights to your home, and any equity you may have.

- **Get Promises in Writing** – Oral promises are not legally binding. Protect your rights with a legal document. Keep copies of all contracts you sign.

- **Report suspicious activity to federal agencies** – Call the Federal Trade Commission, or your state and local consumer protection agencies. This will also help prevent others from becoming victims.

---

26 U.S. Department of the Treasury

- **Contact a legitimate housing or financial counselor to help you work it out** – To find a counselor, contact the U.S. Department of Housing and Urban Development (HUD) at: 1(800)569-4287 or 1(877)483-1515.

 TIP: *Always Proceed with Caution When Dealing with Anyone Offering to Help You Modify Your Mortgage or Avoid Foreclosure.*

Myth # 46: Foreclosure Sales Offer a Good Opportunity to Buy a House at a Bargain Price

Fiction: It's a very hard, if not impossible, to find a bargain at a foreclosure sale. In order to compete at the auction, you must have a cashier's check for the amount of your bid. If you are the successful bidder, you will receive the property in "as-is" condition, which could include someone living in the property. There may also be other liens on the property.

Foreclosure sales begin with a minimum bid that includes the loan balance, any accrued interest, attorney fees, and all other related costs. The minimum bid is typically more than the market value of the home. Since buyers are all looking for a bargain, the property usually reverts to the lender and becomes an REO.

There are some additional challenges in buying at auction:[27]

1. You will have limited or no access to the property because it is usually occupied

2. After the sale, you may have to take legal action to evict the residents

3. You will not be able to conduct a property inspection

4. You are responsible for paying any outstanding liens

5. You may have an issue with borrower's right of redemption if you live in a state that allows it

6. The lender will require an all-cash, 30 day close

There many ways to save money when buying a house, but this isn't one of them.

---

27   Reprinted with permission of the Real Estate Buyer's Agent Council (REBAC), a wholly owned subsidiary of the National Association of Realtors. Copyright 2009, REBAC

SECTION 5:
THE ART OF BUYING

The buying process is currently a minefield. Financing is difficult, the market is filled with foreclosures and short sales, prices have not yet stabilized, and economists are projecting that the market won't return to normal until years 2013 to 2115.

This section will give the buyer tips and reveal insider secrets about when and where to buy, what types of offers to make, how to minimize problems after going under contract, what type of down payment is needed, how to handle inspections, what type and how much title insurance to buy, and how to save money on the whole process.

Myth # 47: It is Better to Rent Than Buy

Fiction: There are many reasons to buy. Among them, tax issues loom large.

First: When figuring your federal or state tax returns, you may be able to deduct the interest you pay on your mortgage, as well as your property taxes.

Second: You are building equity because a portion of your mortgage payment goes to principal, which is yours to keep.

Third: If you have a fixed-rate mortgage, your monthly payments will remain stable.

Fourth: Homeownership provides shelter and security for your family and gives you a sense of belonging.

Figure 5.1 presents a rent versus buy comparison example. In this example, your house payment on a $300,000 home with 20 percent down would be significantly less than rent for the same house. For illustrative purposes, we used a 28 percent tax rate and estimated property taxes to be 1 percent of the purchase price. That will vary, of course, depending on local rates and your tax situation.

Figure 5.1: Rent vs. Buy Comparison Example

	Conventional 20% Down	Conventional 10% Down	FHA 3.5% Down
Purchase Price	$300,000	$300,000	$300,000
Down Payment	60,000	30,000	10,500
Loan Amount	$240,000	$270,000	$289,500
Loan Payment	$ 1,215	$ 1,370	$ 1,465
PMI	0	135	145
Insurance	150	150	150
Property Tax (1%)	250	250	250
Total Payment	1,615	1,905	2,010
Deductions:			
Interest	$ 900	$ 1,010	$ 1,085
Property Tax	250	250	250
Total	$ 1,150	$ 1,260	$ 1,335
x .28% Income Tax Rate = (Tax Savings)	322	352	374
Total Payment	$ 1,615	$ 1,905	$ 2,010
Less Tax Savings	322	352	374
Net Payment	$ 1,293	$ 1,553	$ 1,636
Equivalent Rent	$ 1,900	1,900	1,900
Monthly Savings	$ 607	$ 347	$ 264

You need to talk to your tax advisor about your individual situation. This is just an example to demonstrate the concept. One last point on this issue:

according to the California Association of Realtors, a Harvard University Joint Center of Housing Studies report showed that the median net worth of homeowners is 34 times greater than for renters, and more than half of that wealth came from home equity.

Myth # 48: It is Best to Find the House You Want to Buy Before Listing Your Own House

Fiction: In almost any market, sellers will not accept an offer contingent upon the sale of your current home. It as a waste of time to even write an offer. In addition, you really don't know how much you will net from the sale of your house, so you don't know how much down payment you will have. Therefore, you don't know the amount of loan you can get, and what priced home you can qualify for.

Joe and Brenda were a young couple who owned a condo. They wanted to move up to a single family home, so they contacted our agent, Shirley, to assist them. They told Shirley they were ready to start looking at houses, but Shirley said that it would be better if they sold their condo first. Joe and Brenda felt they knew better, so Shirley relented and took them to see houses in their price range.

The first week they found a house they really liked, so Shirley wrote a full-price offer for them, contingent upon the sale of their condo. They were stunned when the seller refused their offer. The seller said that not only was their condo not sold, it wasn't even on the market!

Undeterred, Joe and Brenda continued their search. Lo and behold, they found another house that they liked. Shirley wrote another offer for them, again contingent upon the sale of their condo. This time, the offer was $90,000 below the asking price because they felt the house was overpriced.

Because of the low offer and the fact that they had a property to sell, a double whammy, the seller didn't even counter their offer. Joe and Brenda didn't really understand why the seller wouldn't negotiate with them. After all, they were honest and trustworthy, and they had good jobs. What was the problem?

After being rejected for the second time, Joe and Brenda had had enough, so they let Shirley put their condo on the market. They priced the property so well; it sold in less than 30 days, with a 45-day closing. They waited until their condo closed, however, before looking for another house.

The buyer had graciously let them rent back for 60 days after the closing. Now that they were in the "flow," Shirley found a house that was even better than the two they had offered on. Because they were no longer contingent buyers, they negotiated an even better price than expected. They closed their new house in 30 days because they were pre-approved and had cash in the bank.

Finally, Joe and Brenda admitted to Shirley that she had been right all along.

Myth # 49: You Don't Have to Compromise When You Buy a House

Fiction: Unless you have unlimited resources, buying a home always involves compromises. Even with unlimited resources, it is not an easy task.

Do you want more bedrooms, even if they are smaller? Would you rather have a smaller house with a large yard, or a larger house with a small yard? Would you forgo a family room to get another bedroom?

Do you see the dilemma? Because you have a limit on the price you can pay, you will have to make those kinds of decisions. Life is a series of compromises, isn't it?

But once you move into your house, all this will be forgotten!

Myth # 50: New Homes are a Better Value

Fiction: The difference between model homes, which you studied to decide on a floor plan, and a production home, which is what you actually get when you don't upgrade, is like night and day. Also, the production house usually doesn't come with landscaping. To find out what the final tab will be, you need to figure in all the costs to upgrade and landscape the property. Often it is more than an equivalent resale house.

Fritz and Gail had recently relocated to our area and were referred to our agent Charlene. Fritz had a high-paying job as an engineer. They had sold their house in Pittsburgh and were ready to buy. Even though Charlene cautioned them about the extra costs associated with a new home, they still insisted that they wanted to buy new.

Charlene took them to all the new tracts in their price range, which was about $500,000. Fritz and Gail finally found a tract they liked, selected a floor plan, and signed a purchase agreement with the builder for a price of $525,000.

That's when the fun began.

First, they were sent to the design center where they were shown exactly what came with the house—very little. Nothing like the model home they had seen. When they began probing, the designer told them the models averaged over $200,000 in upgrades. No wonder they looked so good!

Fritz and Gail found themselves with upgraded carpeting, travertine flooring in the kitchen and baths, upgraded appliances, window coverings, and lighting. By the time they finished, they had spent an extra $55,000, bringing their total to $580,000.

Then Gail asked, "What about landscaping?"

Fritz went limp. Since the builder didn't provide landscaping, they had to contract with an outside landscaping company. Gail also wanted a pool.

Fortunately, their lot was on the small side, typical of new homes. The landscaping was an additional $60,000, bringing their final price to $640,000. Plus, they had to wait until the transaction closed before they could begin work. So when they moved in, they had a dirt lot.

Still, they had their new home.

They could have purchased a similar resale home with the same amenities, including a pool, for about $600,000.

Don't get me wrong; I am not knocking new homes. I know some builders very well. If you really want new, then that is what you should do. Sometimes, new homes are priced well. But it helps to know the whole picture before you make a decision.

 TIP: When buying a New Tract House, Be Sure to Look at a Production House, Not Just the Model, Before Deciding.

Myth # 51: It's Best to Look Only at Homes in Your Price Range

Fiction: Prices of homes are usually negotiable. For example, if you intend to pay no more than $400,000 for a house, your might find yourself looking only at listings from $350,000 to $400,000. But that would be a mistake. It is possible that you would miss out on a house listed at $410,000, with a motivated seller who would negotiate down to $400,000.

Myth # 52: Location is Important When Buying a House

Fact: You can do almost anything to a house. You can add a room, or even a second story, if permitted. You can remodel the kitchen, bathrooms, closets, or family room. You can do almost anything—except move it!

I am sure you have heard that the three most important rules in buying a house are location, location, location. There is a lot of truth to that. If you want a particular school district, the house has to be located within its boundaries. Another factor might be finding a neighborhood with small children. If you have a family, you might want an area that has a low crime rate. You also might want to live close to where you work. If you want a newer home, they are generally found in definite areas of the city. You might want to be near a park.

One thing you don't want is the nicest home in a marginal neighborhood. It is far better to have a marginal home in a good neighborhood. You must also consider that prices vary dramatically with location. Newer, upscale neighborhoods command a higher price.

 TIP: Make Sure You Establish Your Location Parameters Before Looking for a House.

Myth # 53: Always Buy the Best, Most Improved House in the Neighborhood

Fiction: The rule countering this is called the "Principle of Progression."

This means that the lowest-priced home in a neighborhood will appreciate at a higher rate than the highest-priced home. Unless you have money to burn, or just want to show off, you are better off buying a lesser house than the "the biggest one on the block."

Myth # 54: Price is the Most Important Issue When Buying a House

Fiction: Have you heard about terms? Sometimes terms trump price. If you find an owner who can carry the financing, you will save a lot of up-front costs. It is then worth it to pay a little more for the house. Also, the owner might throw in some furniture, maybe even a refrigerator, or washer and dryer, so you won't have to purchase them.

So you see, it's not always about price.

 TIP: Price is Important, But You Always Need to Look at the Big Picture.

Myth # 55: You Can Save Money by Buying a "Fixer-Upper"

Fiction: I could tell you endless horror stories about people buying fixer-uppers, but I won't. Suffice it to say that with these types of properties, it's "caveat emptor"—buyer beware. I have seen so many situations over the years where, after the transaction closed, the buyer found things he didn't anticipate.

For example, one buyer found black mold behind a shower wall. Another, structural damage to the house. Still another, a cracked foundation under the carpeting. If you are going to buy a fixer, you need to be very careful. Make a list of items that need repair and price them out before you buy. Make sure the price you pay makes sense. When you add the repairs to the cost of the house, is it still below a comparable sale?

More often it is not.

TIP: When Buying a "Fixer-Upper," Make Sure You First Get a Thorough Physical Inspection.

If you do decide to buy a fixer-upper, consider living in the property while you make the repairs and do some of them yourself. This creates what we call "sweat equity."

Myth # 56: Always Make a Low-Ball Offer to Get the Best Price

Fiction: Low-ball offers often offend the seller. I have seen many instances where the seller refuses even to respond to a low offer. You end up shooting yourself in the foot. If you use this tactic when buying a house, you could be lumped in a category of buyers called "bottom feeders." A pretty negative term.

Even if the seller does respond to your offer, he will have his back up, and it will be difficult to negotiate. You would be far better off making a reasonable offer.

George was a single man in his 40s. He had previously bought and sold two houses, so he considered himself an expert. Of course, he was an engineer. Don't misunderstand me; some of my best friends are engineers. But too often they believe they know everything and can solve every problem. They are among the toughest clients for a Realtor to work with.

One day George wandered into an open house where he met our agent, Donna. She sat down with him to find out his requirements, and they made an appointment for the following weekend.

When the weekend came, Donna drove George around to see six houses she thought would interest him. She was right. He found one he really liked, so they drove back to the office to write an offer.

The house was listed for $595,000. While Donna was filling out the paperwork (we like to say "paperwork" rather than "contract"; it has a better ring), she asked George what price he wanted to offer. She was taken aback when he said $500,000.

She tried unsuccessfully to dissuade him, eventually writing the offer for $500,000.

The seller refused to respond, saying that the buyer clearly wasn't serious.

George was shocked. "Doesn't the seller know I am a well-qualified buyer?"

Donna didn't reply. Instead, she referred him to another agent, who was desperate enough to work with a "bottom feeder."

Myth # 57: Always Take Time to Think it Over Before Making an Offer

Fiction: Thinking it over is probably the most common objection to writing an offer. In fact, there are many real estate trainers who teach agents how to handle this very delicate objection. The problem is, it works to the detriment of the buyer. Often, a buyer misses out on a good house because, while he is thinking it over, someone else buys it. You should know whether or not you want to buy the house, and act accordingly. He who hesitates, etc, etc.

One of our agents, Jennifer, had been working with an older couple from Santa Barbara, Greg and Roberta. They would drive down the 100+ miles to our area once a month on a weekend to look at property. They were very particular about what they wanted, so showing them property wasn't an easy task.

One Saturday, they got lucky and found a house that was almost exactly what they were looking for. It was in excellent condition and was priced well at $570,000. Barbara knew that homes in this price range were selling quickly, especially those in such great condition.

She told Greg and Roberta that the house would probably sell that weekend, so if they wanted it, they should put in an offer right away.

Greg and Roberta said that they didn't want to rush, they would get back to Jennifer on Monday. Apparently, they thought her sense of urgency was just sales hype.

When they called Jennifer on Monday to say they wanted the house, she had to tell them the house sold on Sunday. Greg and Roberta were shocked, and for four months, stopped looking.

Finally, they called Jennifer and said they were ready to look again. During the next seven months, they visited five times, with no luck.

Then one week after their last visit, Jennifer called to tell them the house they had first wanted had come back on the market and asked if they would like to see it. Of course, they said yes and drove down the next day, a Saturday.

Jennifer took them to see the house, and it just reaffirmed their desire. They didn't want to miss out again, so they had Jennifer write a full-price offer, which was $610,000. This time their offer was accepted, and when the transaction closed, Greg and Roberta were extremely happy. They felt fortunate to have the house they really wanted, even though it cost $40,000 more.

They had learned their lesson.

Myth # 58: When Getting a Loan, Always Make Your Offer Subject to Appraisal and Loan Approval

Fact: If you don't do that, and the appraisal comes in lower than your contract price, you will be obligated to pay the difference in cash. The only other alternative would be to back out of the sale, which will put your deposit in jeopardy. This is a lose-lose situation that can easily be prevented by including an appraisal and loan contingency in the contract. Don't leave home without it!

It is also important to know the steps in the home-buying process. Even more important is that they be done in the following order:

1. **Select a Realtor** – use the method described in Myth # 13.

2. **Select a lender** – ask your Realtor for a referral, or use the same method you'd use to choose a Realtor.

3. **Get pre-approved by your lender** – find out what you really can buy.

4. **Determine your house criteria** – focus on what you really need (bedrooms, baths, etc.). Separate your wish list from your must-have list. Your Realtor can help you with this step.

5. **Select a neighborhood or neighborhoods** – remember: location, location, location.

6. **Look at homes** – your Realtor will show you homes in your price range that meet your criteria.

7. **Compare homes** – before making a decision, compare your wants and needs with each house you like. Look at the long-term costs. (Older homes will generally require more maintenance.)

8. **Make an offer** – when you have selected a house, your Realtor will write an offer, usually with a pre-printed Purchase Agreement. If you really want the house, make a good offer, don't low-ball. (See Myth # 56.) If there are multiple offers, consider a price escalation clause. (See Myth # 63.)

9. **Negotiate the sale** – if your offer is full price, then the only negotiating will be on terms. If you are not involved with competing offers, you may have to make one or more counter-offers to agree with the seller on price and terms.

10. **Review Seller's Disclosures** – this may include a Transfer Disclosure Statement, a Natural Hazards Disclosure Statement, and a Preliminary Title Report (Prelim), depending on where you are. The Prelim is important because it contains matters of record that specifically affect the property, like liens, easements, and property taxes. Also, you should have requested a termite clearance, so review the termite report.

11. **Conduct a physical inspection** – hire a reliable, qualified home inspector to do the physical inspection, and be present while it is being done. That way you have a firsthand look at the items the inspector will note. Depending on what he finds, he may recommend further inspections, like a roof inspection, a geological inspection, a structural inspection, or an environmental inspection.

12. **Request repairs** – your Realtor will write a repair request based on the items you want to be repaired, and deliver it to the seller.

13. **Conduct a final walk-through** – before closing, check to see if the requested repairs have been made, and that the property is in the same condition as it was when you made your offer.

14. **Close the transaction** – prior to close, request copies of all the documents you will be required to sign, and review them, or have your attorney review them. This will include your loan documents, a preliminary HUD-1 Statement, which is an estimate of your closing costs, an initial Escrow Settlement Statement, if you are going to have your property taxes and insurance costs impounded, and a Truth in Lending Statement.

An escrow account is used to collect and hold funds for the purpose of paying property taxes and insurance. Your mortgage company pays these bills for you when they are due. That way, you contribute a smaller monthly amount, instead of having to come up with the whole amount at one time.

Most states have a closing/settlement meeting. The people in attendance will be the buyer, the seller, the title company representative, the closing agent, the escrow agent, and the Realtors. In some cases the attorneys for the parties will also be present. At the closing meeting, you will have to sign all the required documents, including the loan documents, provide proof of insurance, and provide funds for your down payment and closing costs. These funds will have to be in the form of a certified or cashier's check.

In states that don't have closing meetings, like California, you will sign documents at the office of a neutral third party (escrow company), and they will handle the closing from there. For that, you do not need to be present.

After the title has recorded, you will receive the keys. The house is now yours. Congratulations!

Myth # 59: It is Best to Give the Other Party Plenty of Time to Respond to Your Offer

Fiction: This is a no-no in the world of negotiation. You do not want the other party to have lots of time to think over your offer, or counter-offer, because they will conjure up of all kinds of reasons not to accept it. The longer they have, the more reasons will appear.

Most standard pre-printed Purchase Agreements have a standard three-day limit, unless you manually change it. Here is a better way:

1. Give the other party only 24 hours to respond—unless there is a reason why they can't.

2. If your agent is presenting the offer in person, have your offer (counter-offer) expire upon presentation. You will have a better chance of being successful.

Another thing, with a long response time, you run the risk of competing offers appearing.

Myth # 60: If the House Looks Good, and the Seller's Disclosures are Fine, You Can Save Money by Not Paying for a Physical Inspection

Fiction: No matter how good it looks, you are probably not an expert in evaluating physical properties of a house. Hidden pitfalls lurk everywhere. This could be the topic of another book. If something major shows up, like a cracked slab, after you own the property, you will be on the hook for it.

For most homes, a good inspection will cost about $500.

Why take a chance?

 TIP: Even If You are Buying a New House, Hire a Professional Physical Inspector.

Myth # 61: When Buying a Title Policy, You Only Need to Insure for the Amount of Your Loan

Fiction: If you have ever purchased a home before, you are probably familiar with the benefits of title insurance. But it won't hurt you to hear it again....

What is Title Insurance?

Title insurance is a policy that protects you against losses that occur when title to a property is not free and clear of defects (like liens.). There are two types of title insurance policies, a Lender's Policy and an Owner's Policy. Lenders require title insurance as a condition of your loan, and require it only for the amount of your loan. A Lender's Policy does not protect you, only the lender. Also, the prior owner's policy does not protect you

If you want to protect yourself from claims against your new home, you will need an Owner's Policy. Such a policy insures the buyer for the full purchase price of the property, which is the title company limit. Figure 5.2 outlines 20 reasons why you need title insurance.

Who Pays For the Title Policy?

Depending upon the region, the title premium may be paid by the buyer or the seller, or split between the two; — that is a matter of local custom, and not set by law. The buyer typically pays for the Lender's Policy, though.

For example, in Northern California, the buyer pays for the Homeowner's policy, but in Southern California, the seller pays.

Title companies are in the business to make sure your rights and interests to the property are clear, that transfer of title takes place efficiently and correctly, and that your interests as a homebuyer are protected to the maxim degree possible. The life of a title search is illustrated in Figure 5.3.

Figure 5.2: 20 Reasons for Title Insurance[28]

1. Title insurance will protect you against a loss on your home or land due to a title defect.
2. A deed or mortgage in the chain of title may be a forgery.
3. Claims constantly arise due to marital status and validity of divorces.
4. A deed or mortgage may have been made by an incompetent or under-aged person.

---

28 Reprinted with permission of California Title Company

Figure 5.2: 20 Reasons for Title Insurance (continued)

5. A deed or mortgage made under an expired power of attorney may be void.

6. A deed or mortgage may have been made by a person with the same name as the owner.

7. A child born after the execution of a will may have interest in the property.

8. Title transferred by an heir may be subject to a federal estate tax lien.

9. An heir or other person presumed dead may appear and recover the property or an interest.

10 A judgment regarding the title may be voidable because of some defect in the proceeding.

11. By insuring the title you can eliminate delays when passing your title on to someone else.

12. Title insurance reimburses you for the amount of your covered loss.

13. Title insurance helps speed negotiations when you're ready to sell or obtain a loan.

14. A deed or mortgage may be voidable if signed while the grantor was in bankruptcy.

15. Claims have risen dramatically over the last 30 years.

16. There may be a defect in the recording of a document upon which your title is dependent.

17. Title insurance covers attorneys' fees and court costs.

18. Many lawyers protect their clients as well as themselves, by procuring title insurance.

19. A deed or mortgage may have been procured by fraud or duress.

20. A title policy is paid in full by the first premium for as long as you own the property.

Figure 5.3: The Life of a Title Search[29]

Customer Service Verifies Legal Property Description
& How Title to Real Property is Held

Preliminary Order & Title Search are Opened

Preliminary Search of Real Property

Title Search Examines Real Property Records,
General Index Records & Tax Records

Examiner Reviews Complete Search Package
& Writes Preliminary Report
ê

Preliminary Title Information is Entered into Computer
& Preliminary Report Prepared

Messenger Service Delivers Preliminary Reports to Escrow & Lenders

New Documents, Demands & Statements or
Information Submitted to Title Company

Documents are Recorded, Confirmation of Recording is
Received & Liens of Record are Paid Off

Title Officer Writes Title Policies

Data Processor Prepares Final Title Policies

Title Policies Released to Client

---

29   Reprinted with permission of California Title Company

Myth # 62: Always Have a Home Warranty When Purchasing a House

Fact: It may be the best home-purchase money you will ever spend. The cost of a home warranty will vary by state, but to give you an idea, here is the cost for California from First American Home Buyers Protection Corporation. A basic policy for a home of 5,000 square feet or less is $270.* This will cover the plumbing, wiring, built-in appliances, garage door opener, and much more, for one year from the date you close. You can also add coverage for central air-conditioning, refrigerator, washer and dryer, and pool/spa for an additional fee for each item. If you have a problem after you move in, you pay a small service charge for each issue and First American will repair or replace the item.[30] Check service contract for covered items and exclusions.)

To find the cost in your state, or for more information, go to www.firstam.com/warranty. If you so desire, you can also obtain roof coverage from various companies. On a home of less than 5,000 square feet, the typical cost is around $200 for a one-year policy.

> TIP: If the Seller Pays for a Home Warranty for the Buyer, He Can Buy a Seller's Policy That Will Cover Him During the Listing Period. (In California, the Cost for a Seller's Policy is 74 Cents per Day.)*

Roger and Cindy were excited about buying their first home. They had saved enough for a down payment and were ready to start looking. They were referred to our agent, Joyce, to assist them in their quest. After looking for three weeks, they found a home that suited their needs. The owner was selling the home as-is, and would make no repairs. They made an offer, and after several counter-offers, the seller agreed to a price of $425,000.

Roger and Cindy had saved $50,000, which barely covered their down payment and closing costs. They had no money for repairs.

During the final walk-through, Roger and Cindy found that the dishwasher was not working and the hot water heater was leaking. Both of these items had been fine when they conducted their physical inspection. They were deflated because they were buying the home as-is, and had no

---

30 Reprinted with permission of First American Home Buyers Protection Corporation

money to cover these costs. Then Joyce informed them that the seller had purchased seller's coverage when he bought the home warranty. The seller would just have to pay a small service fee to fix the problem. The home warranty company repaired the dishwasher and replaced the hot water heater.

Roger and Cindy could now close on their new home with no worries, and a one-year home warranty as a bonus.

*Rates subject to change.

Myth # 63: When Faced with Competing Offers, the Buyer's Best Strategy is to Write a Full-Price Offer

Fiction: In a multiple-offer situation, there may be several full-price offers, as well as offers above asking price. How do you compete with that?

Here's how. Write your offer at full price, but include a price escalation clause that states you will pay $1,000 above the highest price offered, provided that the seller shows you written proof of that offer. Try that on your next multiple-offer situation.

 TIP: Another Strategy to Use in a Multiple-Offer Situation is to Write a Letter to the Seller, Telling Him Everything You "Love" About His House, and Include it with Your Offer.

Myth # 64: It's Best to Try to Time Your House Purchase with the Bottom of the Market

Fiction: First of all, it is almost impossible to predict the bottom. Second, you won't know it's the bottom until that moment has passed, and prices are consistently on the rise. Third, you run the risk of rising interest rates, which usually accompany recoveries. The best time to buy a house is just before the bottom, but since you won't know when that is, don't be so concerned about hitting it. Bottom line: Buy when you want to or have to, and don't worry about the lowest possible price. In the long run, you will be fine.

Myth # 65: Always Make the Smallest Earnest Money Deposit You Can

Fiction: That strategy may backfire. You want to impress the seller with your qualifications, particularly in multiple-offer situations. A rule of thumb for earnest money deposits is 3 percent of the selling price—unless you are buying FHA or VA. Again, if you are in a multiple-offer situation, think about making your deposit 10 percent of the purchase price. That will get the seller's attention!

Myth # 66: If I Decide Not to Buy a House That I Have Under Contract, I Can Always Get My Deposit Back.

Fiction: Always be careful when you hear "never" or "always." Once you have removed all your contingencies, your deposit belongs to the seller. Unless he has some compelling reason to return it to you, your money is lost. Earnest money deposits were created for this very reason. The seller has his property off the market while you were under contract, so this is a means of compensating him.

If, however, you decide not to buy a house because of a contingency, then you are normally entitled to get your deposit back, less costs.

(Note: To obtain a FREE report,"99 Questions and Answers about Buying a Home," go to page 211.)

Section 6:
SELLING LESSONS

Selling is always a challenge, but in this market, and for years to come, it will test the ingenuity of many sellers and Realtors. As we have said before, economists are predicting unstable real estate conditions until at least 2013.

This section will help you by providing tips and insider secrets on topics such as:

- How to determine a listing price
- The best time to sell
- How to handle marketing
- The type of listing agreement to use
- How to handle offers and counter-offers
- What to do about repairs
- What disclosures you need

Myth # 67: I Should Wait for Prices to Increase Before Selling

Fiction: This assumes that you don't have an urgent reason to sell, like a job transfer, which would dictate timing. But if you really intend to wait for prices to go up, you may be old and gray before that happens. In the near term, prices are expected to fall, and , as we said before, experts are predicting that it will be years 2013 to 2015 before we return to anywhere near normal. (Maybe, instead, we will have a new normal.)

Besides, if you are ready to buy another house, it really doesn't matter. The price of both houses will go up and down together.

> *TIP: When Prices Increase, the Differential between Your House and the More Expensive One You are Buying Will Only Grow Greater.*

Myth # 68: Never Offer Your House for Sale Near the End of the Year

Fiction: This may be one of the best times of year to do it. You have the least amount of competition, since everyone thinks alike, and few others enter the market.

In addition, buyers who are looking at that time are usually motivated, or they wouldn›t be house hunting during the holidays.

People facing a job transfer have to find a new home as quickly as possible, no matter the time of year. We have sold homes on Christmas Day. The seller wasn't thrilled about the showing, but he was happy it sold.

Myth # 69: I Should Worry About the Tax Implications of Selling

Fiction: The Federal Tax Relief Act of 1998 allows you to sell your home and exclude $500,000 of the gain if you file a joint return, and $250,000 on a separate return, or for a single taxpayer. To qualify, your home must have been your principle residence for two of the previous five years. You can use this exclusion as often as you can qualify. It is not a one-time event.

The Federal Internal Revenue Service Restructuring and Reform Act of 1998 allows you to pro-rate the $500,000 or $250,000 exclusion for unexpected circumstances such as a job transfer, illness, or hardship, where you are forced to sell before the two-year requirement was met.

Some of these federal tax benefits are available at the state level, also.

> *TIP: Before Selling, Check with Your Tax Professional for Your State's Tax Rules.*

Myth # 70: It is All Right to List Your House High; You Can Always Come Down

Fiction: The first two weeks that a properly is on the market are crucial. That's when every agent who has a buyer in your price range is exposed to your property. However, if your price is too high, it will be invisible to many prospective buyers who are shopping in the price range where your house should be. Your property will not show up on the agent's MLS search because it will be beyond their upper price limit.

For example, if your home's value is $400,000 and you list it for $475,000, agents with buyers in the $400,000 range will search the MLS for homes priced to $400,000, or maybe $410,000. They will never see your house.

Buyers who do see your house will be in a higher price range and will be expecting a lot more than your property provides, because you are in the wrong price range. They will look at competing houses that are priced right, and buy one of those. And if you are in a down market, you might be faced with the unfavorable task of "following the market." Your price may never be right because you are always lagging, and it will take you a very long time to sell. With this scenario, your eventual sales price will be below what you might have received if you had priced it right in the first place.

Myth # 71: It's Better to Use an "Open Listing Agreement" When Listing Your House for Sale

Fiction: The problem with this agreement is that it is not exclusive, and can be given to many agents at the same time. In addition, the owner can still sell the property himself and not pay a commission to anyone. I don't know many agents who would work hard to sell such a property when his efforts could end up producing no income. As a seller, you should want someone who is committed to getting you the highest price for your property. This type of listing agreement will not accomplish that. You will end up shooting yourself in the foot, again.

A much better plan is to use an "Exclusive Right to Sell" agreement. That way you create an agency relationship with your broker, resulting in someone working exclusively for you. He will be motivated, because he will get paid no matter who sells the property. Thanks to increased exposure to buyers, you will get the highest possible price for your property.

> *TIP: When Selling Your Home, Don't Use Either an Open Listing Agreement or an Exclusive Agency Agreement. Always Use an Exclusive Right to Sell Agreement.*

Myth # 72: When Listing Your House, You Should Always Try to Negotiate a Lower Commission

Fiction: This is another case where you can be pennywise and pound foolish. If your goal is to net the most money you can from the sale of your house, it will be hard to accomplish that by cutting the income of the one person who can make it happen— your Realtor.

Assuming that you negotiate a 5 percent commission, your Realtor will split that with the selling broker. It will be advertised on the Multiple Listing Service (MLS) as a 2.5 percent fee to the selling agent. If there were another comparable property in the MLS at a 3 percent fee, which property do you think would generate the most activity and, therefore, attain the highest price?

> *TIP: If You Really Want to Generate the Highest Price, Increase Your Agent's Commission.*

Myth # 73: You Don't Need a Sign or a Lock Box to Sell Your House

Fiction: True only if you don't want to get the highest price. Without a sign, people in the area won't know it's for sale. Without a lock box, your house is off the market whenever you are not home, because no one can get in to show it. A lock box is critical to your success.

While we're on that subject, it's important to know the correct steps in the selling process. They should be completed in the following order:

1. **Select a Realtor**: Use the method described in Myth # 13 and don't start without one.

2. **Establish a listing price:** Have your Realtor prepare a "Comparative Market Analysis" (CMA). Analyze it with your Realtor to find the

right price. This will save you money if you don't want to pay for an expensive appraisal. Remember, the pricing decision is always yours, but lean on your Realtor's expertise.

3. **Stage your home:** Have your Realtor show you what needs to be done to present your house in the best possible light. You can also hire a staging company to do this. For more information on staging, see Myth # 74.

4. **Estimate your net proceeds from the sale:** Have your Realtor assist you in establishing your closing costs. This could include the following:

   - Title Insurance Premium
   - Transfer Taxes
   - Termite Inspection and Repairs
   - Recording Fees
   - Broker Commission
   - Attorney Fees
   - Escrow Fees
   - Homeowner Association Transfer Fees
   - Home Warranty
   - Natural Hazard Disclosure Statement

   You also need to ascertain the payoff balance on your loan. Then subtract all these costs, plus your loan balance, from the estimated sales price. That will be your net proceeds, which is good to know ahead of time. This is especially important if you intend to buy another house. You need to know how much you'll have to work with.

5. **Develop a marketing plan:** Ask your Realtor to prepare a customized marketing plan for your house. Many larger companies have a standard marketing plan that your Realtor can customize. The plan will include:

   - Placing the property in the MLS
   - Conducting an office caravan

- Holding a broker preview

- Placing a sign and lock box on the property

- Placing ads in newspapers and real estate magazines

- Placing the property on Internet sites like www.realtor.com

6. **Prepare required disclosures**: Your Realtor will assist you in determining which disclosures are required. It varies from state to state, but almost always will include a Natural Hazards Disclosure Statement and a Transfer Disclosure Statement.

7. **Negotiate offers:** Again, with your direction, your Realtor will handle negotiations for you. This may involve one or more counter-offers each time.

8. **Conduct required inspections:** This will vary by state and buyer, but usually will include a termite inspection. Your Realtor can recommend a reliable pest control company.

9. **Make repairs**: Ask your Realtor to assist you in determining which buyer-requested repairs to make. A general guideline is that if it's a safety issue, it should be repaired. The rest is up to you. (Some repairs may be required by your contract.)

10. **Attend the closing:** To insure a smooth closing, your Realtor will monitor the closing process and coordinate with the attorneys and/or escrow. If you are in a state that doesn't use escrow companies, you must attend the closing and sign documents.

After the transaction is closed, you will receive a check for your net proceeds. Congratulations!

Myth # 74: Before Putting it on the Market, it's Best to Have Someone Stage Your House

Fact: You want your house to be in the best possible condition for prospective buyers. One of the best things you can do is let the sun in. Buyers like a light and bright house. Keep the shades and drapes open. Replace all your light bulbs with higher wattage.[31]

---

31 Copyright National Association of Realtors, used with permission

The next thing to do is to de-clutter. Go for the neat look. Clean off counter tops, organize your closets, rearrange furniture to make rooms look larger, and put clothes away.

Then look at the outside of your house. That is the first thing the buyer sees. We have had buyers who refused to look at a house—just because of the exterior appearance. Curb appeal is a very important part of staging. Make sure the landscaping is clean and neat. Add flowers if necessary. Touch up any needed paint. Remove anything that doesn't need to be there. Look at your house from a buyer's prospective.[32] For more information on staging, go to www.realtor.org.

Mark and Julie had their house on the market for 90 days without an offer. When the listing expired, they contacted our agent, Margie, to find out why their house hadn't sold. Margie came by for a tour. What she saw was clutter everywhere, way too much furniture, unmade beds, dirty sinks, and the list goes on.

Later, Margie told Mark and Julie that if they listened to her and did exactly what she suggested, she could sell their house. Energized, Mark and Julia promised they would listen to Margie.

She explained there were only two reasons why a house won't sell, price and condition, and their house was priced right. Mark said, "That leaves condition?"

Margie said "that's right", but told him that before they put the house on the market, she wanted them to hire a professional staging company. This was a very large job, so Margie figured a professional was needed. Mark and Julie agreed, and hired a company Margie recommended.

The staging company sent Sylva, their top staging expert, to see Mark and Julie. After Sylvia went through the house, she came up with a long list of needed chores. She sat down with Mark to explain the list and lay out a plan. Over the next two weeks, under Sylvia's supervision, Mark and Julie worked hard to finish the tasks. When they were done, they called Margie.

After she arrived, Margie almost didn't recognize the house. The exterior was painted, and the front yard trimmed and neat. Inside, a lot of furniture

32 Copyright National Association of Realtors, used with permission

had been removed. There was no clutter anywhere. All the beds were made, and the sinks sparkled. The closets were neat. It was amazing. Sylvia had done her job well. Margie then said, "I think we are ready."

They put the house on the market. Margie held an office caravan and a broker preview. A week later, they received an acceptable offer, and it closed in 45 days.

Margie was their hero!

Myth # 75: You Should Request That Your Agent Conduct Open Houses

Fiction: Think about it. What are the odds that a buyer driving down the street, knowing nothing about your house, will come to your open house and find his dream home? I wouldn't bet on it. As a matter of fact, statistics show that fewer than 2 percent of sales occur at open houses.

Your agent would be far better off spending that four hours prospecting for a buyer.

Myth # 76: When Someone is Showing Your House, You Should Stay Around to Answer Questions

Fiction: Realtors are trained to sell. You are not. The best thing you can do is leave. I have seen many potential sales derailed by overzealous sellers.

Let the professionals handle it.

Rod and Diane had their house listed with our agent, Robert. Rod was in construction and worked long hours, so he wasn't home much. Robert had priced the house at $550,000, which was right at market value. He held a broker's preview, generating a lot of interest.

During the first two weeks, there were 15 showings, but no offers. Ten more showings in subsequent weeks failed as well.

Robert was puzzled. The house was priced right; there was lots of interest, but no offers. That didn't make sense.

One day, he received a call from an agent friend, Steve, who told Robert what had happened to him when he showed the house. Steve said the owner,

Diane, followed them around while he was showing, trying to sell his buyer on the best features. She never stopped talking. The final straw was when Diane told the buyers that they had removed some of the kitchen cabinets to make way for a wine cooler and trash compactor.

It turns out that Steve's clients didn't drink and weren't thrilled about the trash compactor, either. What they wanted was a lot of kitchen cabinets. Diane had destroyed any chance of Steve's selling the house.

Steve thought Robert ought to know what was happening.

Robert called some of the other agents who had shown the property, and each and every one had the same story. Their buyers could hardly wait to get out of the place. That night, Robert met with Rod and Diane. He told them that although he appreciated the fact that Diane wanted to help, it would be better during showings if she wasn't home. He asked her to leave the selling to the Realtors.

Diane reluctantly agreed.

Within a week, they received a full-price offer, and the transaction closed 60 days later.

Myth # 77: When Selling Your Home, Never Take the First Offer

Fiction: We have found over the years that, more often than not, the first offer turns out to be the best. The buyers really like the house and want to move on it without delay.

What happens is that the sellers start having second thoughts, imagining they may have priced it too low. Suddenly, they want to wait for something better.

If the first offer looks good and is acceptable to you, seriously consider taking it. Don't wait for that pie in the sky. It may never happen.

One of our agents, Molly, listed a house belonging to her clients, Harry and Maureen, for $650,000. It was a nice four-bedroom house in a good neighborhood. But Harry had a job transfer to another city so they had to move.

The first week, they received an offer for $635,000. The housing market was just starting to turn down, so Molly told them they should seriously consider it.

Because they received an offer so fast, as we have seen many times before, Harry wanted to wait for a better offer. They countered back at full price. Of course, they lost the buyer.

Two months passed without another offer. Harry was already working at his new job in Cleveland and coming home every other weekend. In the meantime, the market was deteriorating, so Molly suggested they lower the price, which they did. The new price was $618,000. Another fruitless month went by with no offers, so they reduced the price further, to $600,000. Their living situation was bad and they were desperate to sell.

They finally received an offer for $525,000, which Molly negotiated up to $550,000. The buyer was well qualified, so the transaction closed 45 days later, almost four months after they turned down their first offer of $635,000.

Myth # 78: When You Have Multiple Offers, Take the Highest Price

Fiction: Two things are just as important as price: terms and buyer qualifications. A high price, with the buyer requesting you to carry all or part of the financing, may not be as good as a lower, all-cash offer.

The same thing applies to a high price with a long period to close. Over time, many things can go wrong. The buyer with the highest price may have a low down payment, with consequent difficulty obtaining financing.

Another buyer may want a large credit for repairs or loan costs, which will effectively lower your price. Also, a buyer may not be qualified, and a late discovery may waste valuable time. There are endless variations.

Can you see how taking the highest price might not always be in your best interest?

 TIP: When You Have Multiple Offers, Evaluate All Factors, Not Just Price.

Myth # 79: You Have to Make All Repairs Requested by the Buyer

Fiction: You should consider repairing all items relating to health and safety. If anything that you disclosed to be in working order is found not to be during the buyer's inspection, you may be obligated to make those repairs.

Beyond that, it is up to you. You are not obligated to do anything else, but you might want to for the sake of the sale. I have, however, seen some outrageous repair requests. Some buyers will use that as a negotiating tool to lower the price.

Always use good judgment when addressing buyer requests.

Also, you might want to consider purchasing a Seller's Home Warranty when you list your house. (See Myth # 62)

Myth # 80: Once You are Under Contract, You Don't Need to Pay Your Mortgage

Fiction: What if it doesn't close, and you end up with a late mortgage payment on your credit report? The bank will give the closing agent a payoff figure for your loan balance through the closing date; so many people don't make their payment while under contract. Big mistake!

Another problem comes if you miss the closing date. You could also end up with a late payment on your credit report.

The only downside is that the bank might not recognize your payment in time to notify the closing agent before you close, and you will have to pursue the bank for a refund. The trade-off is not worth it. Make your payment.

Section 7:
INVESTMENT PRIMER

Buying an investment property can not only provide monthly income, but also serve as a retirement vehicle. But you do need a certain level of knowledge to become an effective investor. Learn everything you can, including terminology from Myth # 90, before you get involved in investing.

It is not my intention to present you with a complete reference manual on how to become an expert investor. There are countless books on that subject. Instead, I will provide you with an overview of the process so that you are at least armed before going into battle.

Myth # 81: It is Hard to Get Started in Investment Real Estate

Fiction: It's only hard if you want it to be. You should start with a small investment, like a duplex or fourplex, to get a feel for the process before you jump in full force. You also should make sure you work with an experienced investment Realtor. That will make the whole experience user-friendly, and remove a lot of the stress.

Gordon and Sue had been in their home for a while, and had managed to save $50,000. They both worked and had a significant income. Their tax advisor suggested they consider buying an investment property to help offset their large tax bill, so they contacted our agent, Janet, who had sold them their house.

Janet was also experienced in small investment properties. The first thing she did was talk with a commercial lender about Gordon and Sue's qualifications, so she knew what she had to work with. The lender told her that they would probably qualify for a property around $200,000, depending on property type and income.

Commercial loans are primarily based on the property. But lenders also want the buyer to have sufficient resources to cover unforeseen expenses. Janet then scheduled an appointment to meet with Gordon and Sue.

After they arrived, Sue said, "Isn't it difficult to buy investment property? We are not sure we can."

Janet told them that people do it every day, and the key was to start small. She recommended starting with a duplex (a two-unit apartment building). She also told them about talking with the lender, and that they would be able to buy in the $200,000 range.

Janet told them she would be holding their hand throughout the entire process, and then explained how it works. She showed them how they could use the interest on the loan, property tax, insurance, and maintenance as a write-off against the income.

They could also depreciate the building portion of the property as an additional deduction. Janet illustrated this by using the example shown in Figure 7.1. Here, they would have an annual positive cash flow of $1,600 ($16,800 income less $15,200 loan payment and expenses). They would also have a $2,600 write-off against ordinary income on their tax returns. Not huge numbers, but a great start in the world of investment.

The best part was, with the tenants rent essentially covering the mortgage and expenses, Gordon and Sue would be building equity in the property without actually paying for it. (Welcome to my world!)

Figure 7.1: Income Property Analysis Example

	Purchase Price:	$200,000
	Down Payments	50,000
	Loan Amount	$150,000
	Gross Income	16,800
	Expenses:	
	Property Tax	$ 2,400
	Insurance	800
	Maintenance	1,200
	Total	$ 4,400
	New Operating Income	$ 12,400
	Loan Payments	10,800
	Cash Flow	$ 1,600
For Taxes:	Property Income	$ 16,800
	Less Expenses	4,400
	Less Interest	9,500
	Less Depreciation	5,500
	Income / (Loss)	$ (2,600)

Gordon and Sue became enthusiastic about the concept, so Janet took them to see a few duplexes in their price range. They found one they liked in a good area and in good condition, so they made an offer.

The property was listed at $205,000, and they made an offer of $200,000, which the seller accepted. Janet guided them through the due diligence process and recommended reliable vendors to assist them. Everything went smoothly, and the transaction closed 60 days after their offer was accepted.

Gordon and Sue were now landlords.

TIP: When Buying an Investment Property, Always Use an Experienced Commercial Realtor.

Myth # 82: A Single Family Home Makes the Best Investment Property

Fiction: The worst investment is one unit; the next worst is two units, and so on. The reason for that is the return on investment and the risk. If you have four units and one is vacant, you still have income from the other three units. But if you have a house (one unit) and it is vacant, you have no income. Also, the income from four units will be proportionately higher than one unit—a house—which will give you a better bottom line.

A lot of commercial properties are rented triple net (NNN), which means the tenant pays the property taxes, insurance, and maintenance costs. That also makes for ease of management.

Following is a summary of investment property types:

1. **APARTMENTS:**

Disadvantages: Very expensive to maintain.

- Very management-intensive. The magic number is 20 units, when it becomes economically feasible to hire a full-time resident manager

- Rehab costs when tenants move out

Advantages: People always need a place to live, so you have fewer vacancies.

- Easier to finance. If you buy two to four units, and live in one, you can obtain favorable owner-occupied financing

- Depending on price, you may be able to obtain a low down payment FHA loan on a two to four unit building if you occupy one unit.

2. **INDUSTRIAL** – Typically a tilt-up concrete warehouse building with some office space. Can be single-tenant or multi-tenant.

Disadvantages: Single-tenant buildings are more risky.

- Difficult to rent if the building was modified to suit a particular tenant.

Advantages: Leases are generally triple-net, so you have no expenses, other than property management.

- The most stable of all property types
- Least management-intensive of all property types. You can basically lease it and forget it

3. OFFICE – Fully improved building with drop ceilings, heating and air-conditioning, private offices, and lobbies. Can be single-tenant or multi-tenant. Recently a new trend has emerged: office condominiums. However, these are usually owner-occupied.

Disadvantages: Difficult to lease. Typically has the highest vacancy rate of any property type.

- Single-tenant buildings are more risky
- More difficult to finance
- Landlord usually pays expenses

Advantages: The exception is the medical office building, which is easier to rent and finance.

4. RETAIL – Can be a single-tenant building (like a restaurant) or a multi-tenant building (like a neighborhood shopping center).

Disadvantages: Difficult to keep rented in bad economic times.

- Need to spend money to maintain exterior appearance

Advantages: Leases are NNN, tenant pays expenses.

- Less management-intensive than offices or apartments

There are also **MIXED-USE** projects, a combination of office and retail, or apartment and retail, which turn out to be the worst of all worlds. You get high maintenance, high expense, and high vacancy.

And then there is **LAND**, which usually generates no income and is considered an "alligator" because you have to keep feeding it. This is generally not good for most people, especially first-time investors, because you have nothing but negative cash flow.

Some people say that land is good if you keep it for the long term.

If you believe that, look what happened to land between 2009 and 2010.

Land prices went down more than 80 percent. You couldn't give it away. In some cases, residential land values were less than zero, because the falling house prices wouldn't even support a land acquisition price of zero! Even if the builders could get the land for free, they would still lose money.

Paul was a very intelligent homeowner. As a matter of fact, he was a member of the American Mensa Society. He came to our office one day looking to buy an investment property. We matched him with our agent Mark, who was an experienced investment broker.

Mark was quite familiar with lender requirements for investment buyers, so he sat down with Paul to find out his investment goals. Paul had a very high six-figure income and $300,000 for a down payment.

Mark explained the different types of investment property:

- Apartments
- Industrial
- Office
- Retail

He told Paul about the advantages and disadvantages of each. After finishing, he asked Paul which he would prefer, and Paul told him he wanted to buy a single-family house.

Mark was startled. He asked Paul if he had not been listening to what he'd just said.

Paul assured him he had, but he still insisted on buying a house.

Mark said, "If I can show you that it makes more sense to buy a commercial property, will you at least consider it?"

Paul said he would.

Mark began explaining the difference between commercial and residential income properties. Using the example outlined in Figure 7.2, he showed Paul the differences in cash flow between single family, apartment, and industrial investments.

Apartments provided $12,000 more net income than single family, and industrial provided $22,000 more. Also, the industrial property lease was triple net (NNN), which means it was net of taxes, insurance, and maintenance. Therefore, the tenant paid all expenses, except property management.

Mark then asked Paul what he now thought about buying a single family house. Paul hesitated a moment, then asked, "What do you have in industrial property?"

After looking at several industrial properties, Paul used his $300,000 to purchase a multi-tenant industrial building at a 7.4 percent cap rate, which provided him a positive cash flow of $19,000. He was a happy camper.

Figure 7.2: *Sample Investment Property Comparison*

	Single Family	Apartment	Industrial
Purchase Price	$1,000,000	$1,000,000	$1,000,000
Down Payment	250,000	300,000	350,000
Loan Amount	$ 750,000	$ 700,000	$ 650,000
Loan Payment	48,000	54,000	55,000
Interest Rate	5%	6.5%	7.5%
Income	60,000	80,000	75,000
Expenses	18,000	20,000	4,000
Net Operating Income	42,000	60,000	71,000
Cap Rate	4.2%	6.0%	7.1%
Net Operating Income	$ 42,000	$ 60,000	$ 71,000
Loan Payment	48,000	54,000	55,000
Cash Flow Before Taxes	($ 6,000)	$ 6,000	$ 16,000
Cash Flow	($ 6,000)	$ 6,000	$ 16,000
Divided by Down Pmt.	250,000	300,000	350,000
Cash-on Cash Return	(3%)	2%	4.6%

Myth # 83: Financing Investment Property is Difficult

Fact: The financial meltdown of 2009 has especially affected availability of funds for investment property. There is virtually no money available for financing land. Retail and office are quite difficult. The only bright spots are apartments and medical offices. For these product types, there is money readily available to qualified buyers. Retail, regular office, and industrial loans are doable, but with great difficulty.

As previously stated, lenders look primarily to the property in evaluating a loan package. They use a debt-to-income ratio for qualifying. That ratio is calculated by dividing the net operating income by the proposed loan payment. In Figure 7.2, the debt-to-income ratio for apartments would be 1.1 ($60,000 divided by $54,000) and the ratio for industrial would be 1.3 ($71,000 divided by $55,000).

The current debt ratio being used by lenders for qualification is around 1.25. Lenders are more comfortable with this because there is a 25 percent cushion for unforeseen problems, such as vacancies or emergency repairs.

If you want to buy investment property, don't let the fear of financing hold you back. It can be done.

Myth # 84: Managing Investment Property is Simple; I Can Do It Myself

Fiction: If you've never done it before, this can be a time-consuming and expensive education. There are many facets involved:

- Knowing how to repair anything from a toilet to an air-conditioner
- Collecting rents
- Evicting tenants
- Legal issues dealing with tenants
- Screening tenants
- Knowing whom to call in emergencies
- Paying all the expenses on time
- Maintaining properties to comply with city codes
- Dealing with government agencies

Learning on the job is not the best way to go. If you really want to do it yourself, consider a triple-net, multi-tenant industrial building. Otherwise, hire a competent property management company,

One of our investment agents, Allen, sold an eight-unit apartment building to his clients, Barry and Karen. After the transaction closed, he asked if they would like recommendations for a property management company.

Barry replied that it wasn't all that difficult; he was going to do it himself.

Allen cautioned him about the pitfalls of personally managing the property, but Barry was insistent. Wishing them good luck, Allen told them to call him if he could be of help.

About seven months later, Allen received a call from Barry. He sounded rattled and out of breath. Allen asked what was wrong, and Barry talked non-stop for 20 minutes.

Barry told him that the very first week, they received a call from a tenant at midnight on Sunday. His toilet was overflowing and flooding his apartment.

A sleepy Barry got dressed and rushed over to fix the problem. It turns out that he couldn't, so he turned off the water to the toilet and told the tenant he would have a plumber repair it the next day. Now he had to find a plumber.

By the middle of the next month, two of the tenants had not paid their rent. Barry went over to see them. One said he had mailed the check, and the other said he was just laid off from his job and could no longer afford the rent.

Of course, the "check in the mail" never came. Now Barry was in the position of having to evict two of his eight tenants, without a clue about how to do it. In the meantime, he was receiving no income from them. He *was* smart enough, however, to hire an eviction attorney to handle it.

The tenant in unit # 2 knew the ropes. After receiving his Three-Day Notice to Quit or Pay Rent, he filed for bankruptcy. It took five months to get him out of the apartment and required the services of a U.S. Marshall.

The other tenant moved out in 60 days. When Barry inspected unit # 2 after the tenant had left, he was stunned. The window coverings were gone, the carpeting was ruined, and the built-in appliances were destroyed, along with countless other items. In the end it cost over $4,000 to put the unit in rentable condition.

To accomplish this, Barry had to hire all the required contractors and supervise their work.

He then put an ad in the paper and started interviewing prospective tenants. When he began verifying their information, he found that some were lying. Finding good tenants was harder than he'd thought.

The final straw was when he received a call from the Fair Housing Agency of the federal government. Someone had filed a complaint because he didn't rent them an apartment. He had to go to a hearing to defend himself. That's when he called Allen.

Allen asked how he could help, and Barry said he needed a good property management company. He was more than ready to hire one. Not only had he spent too much time away from his job, the stress had become unbearable.

Allen gave him two companies to call, and Barry hired one of them.

Three months later, Allen received a call from Barry. He sounded calm and invited Allen to dinner to show his appreciation for his recommendations.

Barry said it was a huge relief to get the burden of management off his back, and he was now devoting more time to his job. He also said hiring a property manager was one of the best decisions he'd ever made.

Myth # 85: It Doesn't Matter Where the Property is Located if the Numbers Make Sense

Fiction: Remember the three rules for buying real estate—location, location, location? Well, they apply even more to investment property. It significantly affects value because properties in the best locations (called A locations) command higher rents, which create higher property values.

You can buy a property for less in a marginal or undesirable area, but you will be better off in the long run in a good area. It will be easier to finance and easier to sell when the time comes. Your property will also appreciate faster.

The one thing you want to consider is how far from your home you want the property to be. The rule of thumb for most investors is that the property should be no more than one hour away from their house. Nobody wants to drive for hours just to check on property.

> TIP: Some Sophisticated Investors Say the Hour Away Can Be By Plane.

Myth # 86: Don't Buy a Property if the Rents are Low

Fiction: Investment property values are primarily based on income. As income increases, the market value of the property goes up. Therefore, a property with low rents has the potential to not only increase your income, but the base value of the property as well. It is called in the trade, a "value-added" opportunity. You make money by buying the property and increasing the rents.

> TIP: When Buying a Property with Low Rents, Make Sure the Price is Based on Actual Rents, Not Pro Forma Income.

Myth # 87: A Property That Needs a Lot of Work is Not a Good Buy

Fiction: The principle is similar to fixer-uppers in single-family homes. You need to buy at a price where, after necessary repairs, you can be below market. Commercial property is different, though, because it is strictly an investment. If you know what you are doing, this is a good way to create additional value. Usually the seller either doesn't want to, or can't make these repairs, so you can get a better price.

Myth # 88: Properties with Amenities, Like a Swimming Pool, are More Desirable

Fiction: Typically, swimming pools are found in apartment buildings, which are already high maintenance. The last thing you want, particularly if you are a first-time investor, is a property with high maintenance. Amenities like pools also create additional expenses for supplies, services, and liability insurance.

When you have a property with special features, it is hard to control expenses because so many unforeseen things can go wrong.

Myth # 89: Condo Conversions are a Good Investment

Fiction: The condo conversion market is dead and may never be revived. The whole premise is dependent on selling the converted apartments as condominiums. You know what happened to the housing market in 2009 and 2010. Condominiums were especially hard hit.

There is so much involved in the process. First, you have to figure out what the eventual selling price will be. Next, you have to figure out what your expenses will be, including carrying costs.

Expenses will include:

- Purchase price of property
- Mapping costs
- Legal fees
- Realtor fees
- Rehab costs
- Loan costs and fees
- Processing fees
- Carrying costs
- Marketing costs

You then take the estimated sales price and subtract all expenses, including the purchase price, to find your estimated profit. Now, and for the foreseeable future, that will be a negative number.

Figure 7.3 shows a condo conversion cost analysis example with a typical loss.

Figure 7.3: Sample Condo Conversion Cost Analysis

Estimated Condo Sales Price	$6,000,000
Mapping Costs	90,000
Legal Fees	30,000
Realtor Fees	360,000
Rehab Costs	2,100,000
Loan Costs and Fees	50,000
Carrying Costs	280,000
Marketing Costs	60,000
Processing Fees	10,000
Purchase Price	4,000,000

Total Estimated Expenses	6,980,000

Net Profit / (Loss)	$(980,000)

Myth # 90: It is Not Important to Learn Investment Terminology

Fiction: If you are going to play the game, you need to know the rules. When people talk to you about cap rates, gross rate multiplier, or debt-to-income ratio, and they get your blank stare, it's not a good sign. You could be in a lot of trouble as an investor. You need to know what all the numbers mean, so here is a quick tutorial on important investment terms.

Capitalization Rate (Cap Rate): The percentage of return on investment used to determine the value of income property through capitalization. The cap rate is determined by dividing the Net Operating Income (NOI) by the property price expressed as a percentage.

To illustrate, using the data from Figure 7.1, dividing the net operating income of $12,400 by the sales price of $200,000, gives you a cap rate of 6.2 percent.

The cap rate is the most widely used number for comparing value when buying investment property.

Gross Rate Multiplier (GRM): Another factor used in evaluating investment property. It is calculated by dividing the price by the gross income. In the above example, dividing the price of $200,000 by the gross income of $16,800 would create a GRM of 12.5. Sellers want that number to be high; buyers want it to be low. It's not a reliable indicator of value because it doesn't take into account the property expenses, which can vary widely. But it can tell you whether the price is in the ballpark.

Gross Income: The total income of the property. In Figure 7.1, it is $16,800.

Net Operating Income (NOI): Total income less all expenses, other than mortgage payments. Again, using Figure 7.1, subtracting expenses of $4,400 from income of $16,800 gives you an NOI of $12,400

Debt to-Income Ratio: This number is used by banks to determine how much money to lend on a property. The number is derived by dividing the net income of the property by the loan payment. Using the above example, the annual loan payment would be $10,800 and the net operating income is $12,400. Dividing $12,400 by $10,800 gives you a debt-to-income ratio of 1.15.

Pro Forma Income: Projected income of an investment property, usually based on full occupancy and market rents, not actual income.

Cash-on Cash Return: Net operating income less loan payment, divided by down payment, expressed as a percentage. Using Figure 7.2, dividing $16,000 cash flow for industrial by $350,000 down payment gives you a 4.6% cash-on-cash return.

There is a lot more involved, but the above are terms you must know.

APPENDIX A

Code of Ethics and Standards of Practice of the
NATIONAL ASSOCIATION OF REALTORS®
Effective January 1, 2010

Where the word REALTORS° is used in this Code and Preamble, it shall be deemed to include REALTOR-ASSOCIATE°s.

While the Code of Ethics establishes obligations that may be higher than those mandated by law, in any instance where the Code of Ethics and the law conflict, the obligations of the law must take precedence.

Preamble

Under all is the land. Upon its wise utilization and widely allocated ownership depend the survival and growth of free institutions and of our civilization. Realtors® should recognize that the interests of the nation and its citizens require the highest and best use of the land and the widest distribution of land ownership. They require the creation of adequate housing, the building of functioning cities, the development of productive industries and farms, and the preservation of a healthful environment.

Such interests impose obligations beyond those of ordinary commerce. They impose grave social responsibility and a patriotic duty to which Realtors® should dedicate themselves, and for which they should be diligent in preparing themselves. Realtors®, therefore, are zealous to maintain and improve the standards of their calling and share with their fellow Realtors® a common responsibility for its integrity and honor.

In recognition and appreciation of their obligations to clients, customers, the public, and each other, Realtors® continuously strive to become and remain informed on issues affecting real estate and, as knowledgeable professionals, they willingly share the fruit of their experience and study with others. They identify and take steps, through enforcement of this Code of Ethics and by assisting appropriate regulatory bodies, to eliminate practices which may damage the public or which might discredit or bring dishonor to the real estate profession. Realtors® having direct personal knowledge of conduct that may violate the Code of Ethics involving misappropriation of client or customer funds or property, willful discrimination, or fraud resulting in substantial economic harm, bring such matters to the attention of the appropriate Board or Association of Realtors®. (Amended 1/00)

Realizing that cooperation with other real estate professionals promotes the best interests of those who utilize their services, Realtors® urge exclusive representation of clients; do not attempt to gain any unfair advantage over their competitors; and they refrain from making unsolicited comments about other practitioners. In instances where their opinion is sought, or where Realtors® believe that comment is necessary, their opinion is offered in an objective, professional manner, uninfluenced by any personal motivation or potential advantage or gain.

The term Realtor® has come to connote competency, fairness, and high integrity resulting from adherence to a lofty ideal of moral conduct in business relations. No inducement of profit and no instruction from clients ever can justify departure from this ideal.

In the interpretation of this obligation, Realtors® can take no safer guide than that which has been handed down through the centuries, embodied in the Golden Rule, "Whatsoever ye would that others should do to you, do ye even so to them."

Accepting this standard as their own, Realtors® pledge to observe its spirit in all of their activities whether conducted personally, through associates or others, or via technological means, and to conduct their business in accordance with the tenets set forth below. (Amended 1/07)

Duties to Clients and Customers

Article 1

When representing a buyer, seller, landlord, tenant, or other client as an agent, Realtors® pledge themselves to protect and promote the interests of their client. This obligation to the client is primary, but it does not relieve Realtors® of their obligation to treat all parties honestly. When serving a buyer, seller, landlord, tenant or other party in a non-agency capacity, Realtors® remain obligated to treat all parties honestly. (Amended 1/01)

- **Standard of Practice 1-1**

  REALTORS®, when acting as principals in a real estate transaction, remain obligated by the duties imposed by the Code of Ethics. *(Amended 1/93)*

- **Standard of Practice 1-2**

  The duties imposed by the Code of Ethics encompass all real estate-related activities and transactions whether conducted in person, electronically, or through any other means.

  The duties the Code of Ethics imposes are applicable whether REALTORS® are acting as agents or in legally recognized non-agency capacities except that any duty imposed exclusively on agents by law or regulation shall not be imposed by this Code of Ethics on REALTORS® acting in non-agency capacities.

  As used in this Code of Ethics, "client" means the person(s) or entity(ies) with whom a REALTOR® or a REALTOR®'s firm has an agency or legally recognized non-agency relationship; "customer" means a party to a real estate transaction who receives information, services, or benefits but has no contractual relationship with the REALTOR® or the REALTOR®'s firm; "prospect" means a purchaser, seller, tenant, or landlord who is not subject to a representation relationship with the REALTOR® or REALTOR®'s firm; "agent" means a real estate licensee (including brokers and sales associates) acting in an agency relationship as defined by state law or regulation; and "broker" means a real estate licensee (including brokers and sales associates) acting as an agent or in a legally recognized non-agency capacity. *(Adopted 1/95, Amended 1/07)*

- **Standard of Practice 1-3**

REALTORS°, in attempting to secure a listing, shall not deliberately mislead the owner as to market value.

- **Standard of Practice 1-4**

REALTORS°, when seeking to become a buyer/tenant representative, shall not mislead buyers or tenants as to savings or other benefits that might be realized through use of the REALTOR°'s services. *(Amended 1/93)*

- **Standard of Practice 1-5**

REALTORS° may represent the seller/landlord and buyer/tenant in the same transaction only after full disclosure to and with informed consent of both parties. *(Adopted 1/93)*

- **Standard of Practice 1-6**

Realtors® shall submit offers and counter-offers objectively and as quickly as possible. (Adopted 1/93, Amended 1/95)

- **Standard of Practice 1-7**

When acting as listing brokers, REALTORS° shall continue to submit to the seller/landlord all offers and counter-offers until closing or execution of a lease unless the seller/landlord has waived this obligation in writing. REALTORS° shall not be obligated to continue to market the property after an offer has been accepted by the seller/landlord. REALTORS° shall recommend that sellers/landlords obtain the advice of legal counsel prior to acceptance of a subsequent offer except where the acceptance is contingent on the termination of the pre-existing purchase contract or lease. *(Amended 1/93)*

- **Standard of Practice 1-8**

REALTORS°, acting as agents or brokers of buyers/tenants, shall submit to buyers/tenants all offers and counter-offers until acceptance but have no obligation to continue to show properties to their clients after an offer has been accepted unless otherwise agreed in writing.

REALTORS', acting as agents or brokers of buyers/tenants, shall recommend that buyers/tenants obtain the advice of legal counsel if there is a question as to whether a pre-existing contract has been terminated. *(Adopted 1/93, Amended 1/99)*

- **Standard of Practice 1-9**

The obligation of REALTORS' to preserve confidential information (as defined by state law) provided by their clients in the course of any agency relationship or non-agency relationship recognized by law continues after termination of agency relationships or any non-agency relationships recognized by law. REALTORS' shall not knowingly, during or following the termination of professional relationships with their clients:

1. reveal confidential information of clients; or

2. use confidential information of clients to the disadvantage of clients; or

3. use confidential information of clients for the REALTOR"s advantage or the advantage of third parties unless:

    a. clients consent after full disclosure; or

    b. REALTORS' are required by court order; or

    c. it is the intention of a client to commit a crime and the information is necessary to prevent the crime; or

    d. it is necessary to defend a REALTOR' or the REALTOR"s employees or associates against an accusation of wrongful conduct.

Information concerning latent material defects is not considered confidential information under this Code of Ethics. *(Adopted 1/93, Amended 1/01)*

- **Standard of Practice 1-10**

REALTORS' shall, consistent with the terms and conditions of their real estate licensure and their property management agreement, competently manage the property of clients with due regard for the rights, safety and health of tenants and others lawfully on the premises. *(Adopted 1/95, Amended 1/00)*

- **Standard of Practice 1-11**

REALTORS® who are employed to maintain or manage a client's property shall exercise due diligence and make reasonable efforts to protect it against reasonably foreseeable contingencies and losses. *(Adopted 1/95)*

- **Standard of Practice 1-12**

When entering into listing contracts, REALTORS® must advise sellers/landlords of:

1. the REALTOR®'s company policies regarding cooperation and the amount(s) of any compensation that will be offered to subagents, buyer/tenant agents, and/or brokers acting in legally recognized non-agency capacities;

2. the fact that buyer/tenant agents or brokers, even if compensated by listing brokers, or by sellers/landlords may represent the interests of buyers/tenants; and

3. any potential for listing brokers to act as disclosed dual agents, e.g., buyer/tenant agents. *(Adopted 1/93, Renumbered 1/98, Amended 1/03)*

- **Standard of Practice 1-13**

When entering into buyer/tenant agreements, REALTORS® must advise potential clients of:

1. the REALTOR®'s company policies regarding cooperation;

2. the amount of compensation to be paid by the client;

3. the potential for additional or offsetting compensation from other brokers, from the seller or landlord, or from other parties;

4. any potential for the buyer/tenant representative to act as a disclosed dual agent, e.g., listing broker, subagent, landlord's agent, etc., and

5. the possibility that sellers or sellers' representatives may not treat the existence, terms, or conditions of offers as confidential unless confidentiality is required by law, regulation, or by any confidentiality agreement between the parties. *(Adopted 1/93, Renumbered 1/98, Amended 1/06)*

- **Standard of Practice 1-14**

  Fees for preparing appraisals or other valuations shall not be contingent upon the amount of the appraisal or valuation. *(Adopted 1/02)*

- **Standard of Practice 1-15**

  REALTORS·, in response to inquiries from buyers or cooperating brokers shall, with the sellers' approval, disclose the existence of offers on the property. Where disclosure is authorized, REALTORS· shall also disclose, if asked, whether offers were obtained by the listing licensee, another licensee in the listing firm, or by a cooperating broker. *(Adopted 1/03, Amended 1/09)*

Article 2

REALTORS· shall avoid exaggeration, misrepresentation, or concealment of pertinent facts relating to the property or the transaction. REALTORS· shall not, however, be obligated to discover latent defects in the property, to advise on matters outside the scope of their real estate license, or to disclose facts which are confidential under the scope of agency or non-agency relationships as defined by state law. *(Amended 1/00)*

- **Standard of Practice 2-1**

  REALTORS· shall only be obligated to discover and disclose adverse factors reasonably apparent to someone with expertise in those areas required by their real estate licensing authority. Article 2 does not impose upon the REALTOR· the obligation of expertise in other professional or technical disciplines. *(Amended 1/96)*

- **Standard of Practice 2-2**

  (Renumbered as Standard of Practice 1-12 1/98)

- **Standard of Practice 2-3**

  (Renumbered as Standard of Practice 1-13 1/98)

- **Standard of Practice 2-4**

  REALTORS° shall not be parties to the naming of a false consideration in any document, unless it be the naming of an obviously nominal consideration.

- **Standard of Practice 2-5**

  Factors defined as "non-material" by law or regulation or which are expressly referenced in law or regulation as not being subject to disclosure are considered not "pertinent" for purposes of Article 2. *(Adopted 1/93)*

Article 3

REALTORS° shall cooperate with other brokers except when cooperation is not in the client's best interest. The obligation to cooperate does not include the obligation to share commissions, fees, or to otherwise compensate another broker. *(Amended 1/95)*

- **Standard of Practice 3-1**

  REALTORS°, acting as exclusive agents or brokers of sellers/landlords, establish the terms and conditions of offers to cooperate. Unless expressly indicated in offers to cooperate, cooperating brokers may not assume that the offer of cooperation includes an offer of compensation. Terms of compensation, if any, shall be ascertained by cooperating brokers before beginning efforts to accept the offer of cooperation. *(Amended 1/99)*

- **Standard of Practice 3-2**

  To be effective, any change in compensation offered for cooperative services must be communicated to the other REALTOR° prior to the time that REALTOR° submits an offer to purchase/lease the property. *(Amended 1/10)*

- **Standard of Practice 3-3**

  Standard of Practice 3-2 does not preclude the listing broker and cooperating broker from entering into an agreement to change cooperative compensation. *(Adopted 1/94)*

- **Standard of Practice 3-4**

  REALTORS®, acting as listing brokers, have an affirmative obligation to disclose the existence of dual or variable rate commission arrangements (i.e., listings where one amount of commission is payable if the listing broker's firm is the procuring cause of sale/lease and a different amount of commission is payable if the sale/lease results through the efforts of the seller/landlord or a cooperating broker). The listing broker shall, as soon as practical, disclose the existence of such arrangements to potential cooperating brokers and shall, in response to inquiries from cooperating brokers, disclose the differential that would result in a cooperative transaction or in a sale/lease that results through the efforts of the seller/landlord. If the cooperating broker is a buyer/tenant representative, the buyer/ tenant representative must disclose such information to their client before the client makes an offer to purchase or lease. *(Amended 1/02)*

- **Standard of Practice 3-5**

  It is the obligation of subagents to promptly disclose all pertinent facts to the principal's agent prior to as well as after a purchase or lease agreement is executed. *(Amended 1/93)*

- **Standard of Practice 3-6**

  REALTORS® shall disclose the existence of accepted offers, including offers with unresolved contingencies, to any broker seeking cooperation. *(Adopted 5/86, Amended 1/04)*

- **Standard of Practice 3-7**

  When seeking information from another REALTOR® concerning property under a management or listing agreement, REALTORS® shall disclose their REALTOR® status and whether their interest is personal or on behalf of a client and, if on behalf of a client, their representational status. *(Amended 1/95)*

- **Standard of Practice 3-8**

  REALTORS® shall not misrepresent the availability of access to show or inspect a listed property. *(Amended 11/87)*

- **Standard of Practice 3-9**

  REALTORS® shall not provide access to listed property on terms other than those established by the owner or the listing broker. *(Adopted 1/10)*

Article 4

REALTORS® shall not acquire an interest in or buy or present offers from themselves, any member of their immediate families, their firms or any member thereof, or any entities in which they have any ownership interest, any real property without making their true position known to the owner or the owner's agent or broker. In selling property they own, or in which they have any interest, REALTORS® shall reveal their ownership or interest in writing to the purchaser or the purchaser's representative. *(Amended 1/00)*

- **Standard of Practice 4-1**

  For the protection of all parties, the disclosures required by Article 4 shall be in writing and provided by REALTORS® prior to the signing of any contract. *(Adopted 2/86)*

Article 5

REALTORS® shall not undertake to provide professional services concerning a property or its value where they have a present or contemplated interest unless such interest is specifically disclosed to all affected parties.

Article 6

REALTORS® shall not accept any commission, rebate, or profit on expenditures made for their client, without the client's knowledge and consent.

When recommending real estate products or services (e.g., homeowner's insurance, warranty programs, mortgage financing, title insurance, etc.), REALTORS® shall disclose to the client or customer to whom the recommendation is made any financial benefits or fees, other than real estate referral fees, the REALTOR˙ or REALTOR˙'s firm may receive as a direct result of such recommendation. (Amended 1/99)

- **Standard of Practice 6-1**

  REALTORS˙ shall not recommend or suggest to a client or a customer the use of services of another organization or business entity in which they have a direct interest without disclosing such interest at the time of the recommendation or suggestion. *(Amended 5/88)*

Article 7

In a transaction, REALTORS˙ shall not accept compensation from more than one party, even if permitted by law, without disclosure to all parties and the informed consent of the REALTOR˙'s client or clients. *(Amended 1/93)*

Article 8

REALTORS˙ shall keep in a special account in an appropriate financial institution, separated from their own funds, monies coming into their possession in trust for other persons, such as escrows, trust funds, clients' monies, and other like items.

Article 9

REALTORS˙, for the protection of all parties, shall assure whenever possible that all agreements related to real estate transactions including, but not limited to, listing and representation agreements, purchase contracts, and leases are in writing in clear and understandable language expressing the specific terms, conditions, obligations and commitments of the parties. A copy of each agreement shall be furnished to each party to such agreements upon their signing or initialing. *(Amended 1/04)*

- **Standard of Practice 9-1**

  For the protection of all parties, REALTORS˙ shall use reasonable care to ensure that documents pertaining to the purchase, sale, or lease of real estate are kept current through the use of written extensions or amendments. *(Amended 1/93)*

- **Standard of Practice 9-2**

  When assisting or enabling a client or customer in establishing a contractual relationship (e.g., listing and representation agreements, purchase agreements, leases, etc.) electronically, REALTORS® shall make reasonable efforts to explain the nature and disclose the specific terms of the contractual relationship being established prior to it being agreed to by a contracting party. *(Adopted 1/07)*

Duties to the Public

Article 10

REALTORS® shall not deny equal professional services to any person for reasons of race, color, religion, sex, handicap, familial status, or national origin. REALTORS® shall not be parties to any plan or agreement to discriminate against a person or persons on the basis of race, color, religion, sex, handicap, familial status, or national origin. *(Amended 1/90)*

REALTORS®, in their real estate employment practices, shall not discriminate against any person or persons on the basis of race, color, religion, sex, handicap, familial status, or national origin *(Amended 1/00)*

- **Standard of Practice 10-1**

  When involved in the sale or lease of a residence, REALTORS® shall not volunteer information regarding the racial, religious or ethnic composition of any neighborhood nor shall they engage in any activity which may result in panic selling, however, REALTORS® may provide other demographic information. *(Adopted 1/94, Amended 1/06)*

- **Standard of Practice 10-2**

  When not involved in the sale or lease of a residence, REALTORS® may provide demographic information related to a property, transaction or professional assignment to a party if such demographic information is (a) deemed by the REALTOR® to be needed to assist with or complete, in a manner consistent with Article 10, a real estate transaction or professional assignment and (b) is obtained or derived from a recognized, reliable, independent, and impartial source. The source of such information and any additions, deletions, modifications, interpretations, or other changes shall be disclosed in reasonable detail. *(Adopted 1/05, Renumbered 1/06)*

- **Standard of Practice 10-3**

  REALTORS° shall not print, display or circulate any statement or advertisement with respect to selling or renting of a property that indicates any preference, limitations or discrimination based on race, color, religion, sex, handicap, familial status, or national origin. *(Adopted 1/94, Renumbered 1/05 and 1/06)*

- **Standard of Practice 10-4**

  As used in Article 10 "real estate employment practices" relates to employees and independent contractors providing real estate-related services and the administrative and clerical staff directly supporting those individuals. *(Adopted 1/00, Renumbered 1/05 and 1/06)*

Article 11

The services which REALTORS° provide to their clients and customers shall conform to the standards of practice and competence which are reasonably expected in the specific real estate disciplines in which they engage; specifically, residential real estate brokerage, real property management, commercial and industrial real estate brokerage, land brokerage, real estate appraisal, real estate counseling, real estate syndication, real estate auction, and international real estate.

REALTORS° shall not undertake to provide specialized professional services concerning a type of property or service that is outside their field of competence unless they engage the assistance of one who is competent on such types of property or service, or unless the facts are fully disclosed to the client. Any persons engaged to provide such assistance shall be so identified to the client and their contribution to the assignment should be set forth. *(Amended 1/10)*

- **Standard of Practice 11-1**

  When REALTORS° prepare opinions of real property value or price, other than in pursuit of a listing or to assist a potential purchaser in formulating a purchase offer, such opinions shall include the following unless the party requesting the opinion requires a specific type of report or different data set:

1. identification of the subject property

2. date prepared

3. defined value or price

4. limiting conditions, including statements of purpose(s) and intended user(s)

5. any present or contemplated interest, including the possibility of representing the seller/landlord or buyers/tenants

6. basis for the opinion, including applicable market data

7. if the opinion is not an appraisal, a statement to that effect *(Amended 1/10)*

- **Standard of Practice 11-2**

The obligations of the Code of Ethics in respect of real estate disciplines other than appraisal shall be interpreted and applied in accordance with the standards of competence and practice which clients and the public reasonably require to protect their rights and interests considering the complexity of the transaction, the availability of expert assistance, and, where the REALTOR˚ is an agent or subagent, the obligations of a fiduciary. *(Adopted 1/95)*

- **Standard of Practice 11-3**

When REALTORS˚ provide consultive services to clients which involve advice or counsel for a fee (not a commission), such advice shall be rendered in an objective manner and the fee shall not be contingent on the substance of the advice or counsel given. If brokerage or transaction services are to be provided in addition to consultive services, a separate compensation may be paid with prior agreement between the client and REALTOR˚. *(Adopted 1/96)*

- **Standard of Practice 11-4**

  The competency required by Article 11 relates to services contracted for between REALTORS® and their clients or customers; the duties expressly imposed by the Code of Ethics; and the duties imposed by law or regulation. *(Adopted 1/02)*

Article 12

REALTORS® shall be honest and truthful in their real estate communications and shall present a true picture in their advertising, marketing, and other representations. REALTORS® shall ensure that their status as real estate professionals is readily apparent in their advertising, marketing, and other representations, and that the recipients of all real estate communications are, or have been, notified that those communications are from a real estate professional. *(Amended 1/08)*

- **Standard of Practice 12-1**

  REALTORS® may use the term "free" and similar terms in their advertising and in other representations provided that all terms governing availability of the offered product or service are clearly disclosed at the same time. *(Amended 1/97)*

- **Standard of Practice 12-2**

  REALTORS® may represent their services as "free" or without cost even if they expect to receive compensation from a source other than their client provided that the potential for the REALTOR® to obtain a benefit from a third party is clearly disclosed at the same time. *(Amended 1/97)*

- **Standard of Practice 12-3**

  The offering of premiums, prizes, merchandise discounts or other inducements to list, sell, purchase, or lease is not, in itself, unethical even if receipt of the benefit is contingent on listing, selling, purchasing, or leasing through the REALTOR® making the offer. However, REALTORS® must exercise care and candor in any such advertising or other public or private representations so that any party interested in receiving or otherwise benefiting from the REALTOR®'s offer will have clear, thorough, advance understanding of all the terms and conditions of the offer. The offering of any inducements to do business is subject to the limitations and restrictions of state law and the ethical obligations established by any applicable Standard of Practice. *(Amended 1/95)*

- **Standard of Practice 12-4**

REALTORS® shall not offer for sale/lease or advertise property without authority. When acting as listing brokers or as subagents, REALTORS® shall not quote a price different from that agreed upon with the seller/landlord. *(Amended 1/93)*

- **Standard of Practice 12-5**

REALTORS® shall not advertise nor permit any person employed by or affiliated with them to advertise real estate services or listed property in any medium (e.g., electronically, print, radio, television, etc.) without disclosing the name of that REALTOR®'s firm in a reasonable and readily apparent manner. *(Adopted 11/86, Amended 1/10)*

- **Standard of Practice 12-6**

REALTORS®, when advertising unlisted real property for sale/lease in which they have an ownership interest, shall disclose their status as both owners/landlords and as REALTORS® or real estate licensees. *(Amended 1/93)*

- **Standard of Practice 12-7**

Only REALTORS® who participated in the transaction as the listing broker or cooperating broker (selling broker) may claim to have "sold" the property. Prior to closing, a cooperating broker may post a "sold" sign only with the consent of the listing broker. *(Amended 1/96)*

- **Standard of Practice 12-8**

The obligation to present a true picture in representations to the public includes information presented, provided, or displayed on REALTORS®' websites. REALTORS® shall use reasonable efforts to ensure that information on their websites is current. When it becomes apparent that information on a REALTOR"s website is no longer current or accurate, REALTORS' shall promptly take corrective action. *(Adopted 1/07)*

• **Standard of Practice 12-9**

REALTOR' firm websites shall disclose the firm's name and state(s) of licensure in a reasonable and readily apparent manner. Websites of REALTORS' and non-member licensees affiliated with a REALTOR' firm shall disclose the firm's name and that REALTOR"s or non-member licensee's state(s) of licensure in a reasonable and readily apparent manner. *(Adopted 1/07)*

• **Standard of Practice 12-10**

REALTORS" obligation to present a true picture in their advertising and representations to the public includes the URLs and domain names they use, and prohibits REALTORS' from:

1. engaging in deceptive or unauthorized framing of real estate brokerage websites;

2. manipulating (e.g., presenting content developed by others) listing content in any way that produces a deceptive or misleading result; or

3. deceptively using metatags, keywords or other devices/ methods to direct, drive, or divert Internet traffic, or to otherwise mislead consumers. *(Adopted 1/07)*

• **Standard of Practice 12-11**

REALTORS' intending to share or sell consumer information gathered via the Internet shall disclose that possibility in a reasonable and readily apparent manner. *(Adopted 1/07)*

• **Standard of Practice 12-12**

REALTORS' shall not:

1. use URLs or domain names that present less than a true picture or

2. register URLs or domain names which, if used, would present less than a true picture. *(Adopted 1/08)*

- **Standard of Practice 12-13**

  The obligation to present a true picture in advertising, marketing, and representations allows REALTORS° to use and display only professional designations, certifications, and other credentials to which they are legitimately entitled. *(Adopted 1/08)*

Article 13

REALTORS° shall not engage in activities that constitute the unauthorized practice of law and shall recommend that legal counsel be obtained when the interest of any party to the transaction requires it.

Article 14

If charged with unethical practice or asked to present evidence or to cooperate in any other way, in any professional standards proceeding or investigation, REALTORS° shall place all pertinent facts before the proper tribunals of the Member Board or affiliated institute, society, or council in which membership is held and shall take no action to disrupt or obstruct such processes. *(Amended 1/99)*

- **Standard of Practice 14-1**

  REALTORS° shall not be subject to disciplinary proceedings in more than one Board of REALTORS° or affiliated institute, society, or council in which they hold membership with respect to alleged violations of the Code of Ethics relating to the same transaction or event. *(Amended 1/95)*

- **Standard of Practice 14-2**

  REALTORS° shall not make any unauthorized disclosure or dissemination of the allegations, findings, or decision developed in connection with an ethics hearing or appeal or in connection with an arbitration hearing or procedural review. *(Amended 1/92)*

- **Standard of Practice 14-3**

  REALTORS° shall not obstruct the Board's investigative or professional standards proceedings by instituting or threatening to institute actions for libel, slander, or defamation against any party to a professional standards proceeding or their witnesses based on the filing of an arbitration request, an ethics complaint, or testimony given before any tribunal. *(Adopted 11/87, Amended 1/99)*

- **Standard of Practice 14-4**

  REALTORS° shall not intentionally impede the Board's investigative or disciplinary proceedings by filing multiple ethics complaints based on the same event or transaction. *(Adopted 11/88)*

Duties to REALTORS®

Article 15

REALTORS° shall not knowingly or recklessly make false or misleading statements about competitors, their businesses, or their business practices. *(Amended 1/92)*

- **Standard of Practice 15-1**

  REALTORS° shall not knowingly or recklessly file false or unfounded ethics complaints. *(Adopted 1/00)*

- **Standard of Practice 15-2**

  The obligation to refrain from making false or misleading statements about competitors, competitors' businesses, and competitors' business practices includes the duty to not knowingly or recklessly publish, repeat, retransmit, or republish false or misleading statements made by others. This duty applies whether false or misleading statements are repeated in person, in writing, by technological means (e.g., the Internet), or by any other means. *(Adopted 1/07, Amended 1/10)*

- **Standard of Practice 15-3**

  The obligation to refrain from making false or misleading statements about competitors, competitors' businesses, and competitors' business practices includes the duty to publish a clarification about or to remove statements made by others on electronic media the REALTOR° controls once the REALTOR° knows the statement is false or misleading. *(Adopted 1/10)*

Article 16

REALTORS˚ shall not engage in any practice or take any action inconsistent with exclusive representation or exclusive brokerage relationship agreements that other REALTORS˚ have with clients. *(Amended 1/10)*

- **Standard of Practice 16-1**

  Article 16 is not intended to prohibit aggressive or innovative business practices which are otherwise ethical and does not prohibit disagreements with other REALTORS˚ involving commission, fees, compensation or other forms of payment or expenses. *(Adopted 1/93, Amended 1/95)*

- **Standard of Practice 16-2**

  Article 16 does not preclude REALTORS˚ from making general announcements to prospects describing their services and the terms of their availability even though some recipients may have entered into agency agreements or other exclusive relationships with another REALTOR˚. A general telephone canvass, general mailing or distribution addressed to all prospects in a given geographical area or in a given profession, business, club, or organization, or other classification or group is deemed "general" for purposes of this standard. *(Amended 1/04)*

  Article 16 is intended to recognize as unethical two basic types of solicitations:

  First, telephone or personal solicitations of property owners who have been identified by a real estate sign, multiple listing compilation, or other information service as having exclusively listed their property with another REALTOR˚; and

  Second, mail or other forms of written solicitations of prospects whose properties are exclusively listed with another REALTOR˚ when such solicitations are not part of a general mailing but are directed specifically to property owners identified through compilations of current listings, "for sale" or "for rent" signs, or other sources of information required by Article 3 and Multiple Listing Service rules to be made available to other REALTORS® under offers of subagency or cooperation. *(Amended 1/04)*

- **Standard of Practice 16-3**

Article 16 does not preclude REALTORS® from contacting the client of another broker for the purpose of offering to provide, or entering into a contract to provide, a different type of real estate service unrelated to the type of service currently being provided (e.g., property management as opposed to brokerage) or from offering the same type of service for property not subject to other brokers' exclusive agreements. However, information received through a Multiple Listing Service or any other offer of cooperation may not be used to target clients of other REALTORS® to whom such offers to provide services may be made. *(Amended 1/04)*

- **Standard of Practice 16-4**

REALTORS® shall not solicit a listing which is currently listed exclusively with another broker. However, if the listing broker, when asked by the REALTOR®, refuses to disclose the expiration date and nature of such listing; i.e., an exclusive right to sell, an exclusive agency, open listing, or other form of contractual agreement between the listing broker and the client, the REALTOR® may contact the owner to secure such information and may discuss the terms upon which the REALTOR® might take a future listing or, alternatively, may take a listing to become effective upon expiration of any existing exclusive listing. *(Amended 1/94)*

- **Standard of Practice 16-5**

REALTORS® shall not solicit buyer/tenant agreements from buyers/tenants who are subject to exclusive buyer/tenant agreements. However, if asked by a REALTOR®, the broker refuses to disclose the expiration date of the exclusive buyer/tenant agreement, the REALTOR® may contact the buyer/tenant to secure such information and may discuss the terms upon which the REALTOR® might enter into a future buyer/tenant agreement or, alternatively, may enter into a buyer/tenant agreement to become effective upon the expiration of any existing exclusive buyer/tenant agreement. *(Adopted 1/94, Amended 1/98)*

- **Standard of Practice 16-6**

When REALTORS° are contacted by the client of another REALTOR° regarding the creation of an exclusive relationship to provide the same type of service, and REALTORS° have not directly or indirectly initiated such discussions, they may discuss the terms upon which they might enter into a future agreement or, alternatively, may enter into an agreement which becomes effective upon expiration of any existing exclusive agreement. *(Amended 1/98)*

- **Standard of Practice 16-7**

The fact that a prospect has retained a REALTOR° as an exclusive representative or exclusive broker in one or more past transactions does not preclude other REALTORS° from seeking such prospect's future business. *(Amended 1/04)*

- **Standard of Practice 16-8**

The fact that an exclusive agreement has been entered into with a REALTOR° shall not preclude or inhibit any other REALTOR° from entering into a similar agreement after the expiration of the prior agreement. *(Amended 1/98)*

- **Standard of Practice 16-9**

REALTORS°, prior to entering into a representation agreement, have an affirmative obligation to make reasonable efforts to determine whether the prospect is subject to a current, valid exclusive agreement to provide the same type of real estate service. *(Amended 1/04)*

- **Standard of Practice 16-10**

REALTORS°, acting as buyer or tenant representatives or brokers, shall disclose that relationship to the seller/landlord's representative or broker at first contact and shall provide written confirmation of that disclosure to the seller/landlord's representative or broker not later than execution of a purchase agreement or lease. *(Amended 1/04)*

- **Standard of Practice 16-11**

  On unlisted property, REALTORS° acting as buyer/tenant representatives or brokers shall disclose that relationship to the seller/landlord at first contact for that buyer/tenant and shall provide written confirmation of such disclosure to the seller/landlord not later than execution of any purchase or lease agreement. *(Amended 1/04)*

  REALTORS° shall make any request for anticipated compensation from the seller/landlord at first contact. *(Amended 1/98)*

- **Standard of Practice 16-12**

  REALTORS°, acting as representatives or brokers of sellers/ landlords or as subagents of listing brokers, shall disclose that relationship to buyers/tenants as soon as practicable and shall provide written confirmation of such disclosure to buyers/tenants not later than execution of any purchase or lease agreement. *(Amended 1/04)*

- **Standard of Practice 16-13**

  All dealings concerning property exclusively listed, or with buyer/ tenants who are subject to an exclusive agreement shall be carried on with the client's representative or broker, and not with the client, except with the consent of the client's representative or broker or except where such dealings are initiated by the client.

  Before providing substantive services (such as writing a purchase offer or presenting a CMA) to prospects, REALTORS° shall ask prospects whether they are a party to any exclusive representation agreement. REALTORS° shall not knowingly provide substantive services concerning a prospective transaction to prospects who are parties to exclusive representation agreements, except with the consent of the prospects' exclusive representatives or at the direction of prospects. *(Adopted 1/93, Amended 1/04)*

- **Standard of Practice 16-14**

  REALTORS° are free to enter into contractual relationships or to negotiate with sellers/landlords, buyers/tenants or others who are not subject to an exclusive agreement but shall not knowingly obligate them to pay more than one commission except with their informed consent. *(Amended 1/98)*

- **Standard of Practice 16-15**

  In cooperative transactions REALTORS® shall compensate cooperating REALTORS® (principal brokers) and shall not compensate nor offer to compensate, directly or indirectly, any of the sales licensees employed by or affiliated with other REALTORS® without the prior express knowledge and consent of the cooperating broker.

- **Standard of Practice 16-16**

  REALTORS®, acting as subagents or buyer/tenant representatives or brokers, shall not use the terms of an offer to purchase/lease to attempt to modify the listing broker's offer of compensation to subagents or buyer/tenant representatives or brokers nor make the submission of an executed offer to purchase/lease contingent on the listing broker's agreement to modify the offer of compensation. *(Amended 1/04)*

- **Standard of Practice 16-17**

  REALTORS®, acting as subagents or as buyer/tenant representatives or brokers, shall not attempt to extend a listing broker's offer of cooperation and/or compensation to other brokers without the consent of the listing broker. *(Amended 1/04)*

- **Standard of Practice 16-18**

  REALTORS® shall not use information obtained from listing brokers through offers to cooperate made through multiple listing services or through other offers of cooperation to refer listing brokers' clients to other brokers or to create buyer/tenant relationships with listing brokers' clients, unless such use is authorized by listing brokers. *(Amended 1/02)*

- **Standard of Practice 16-19**

  Signs giving notice of property for sale, rent, lease, or exchange shall not be placed on property without consent of the seller/landlord. *(Amended 1/93)*

- **Standard of Practice 16-20**

  REALTORS*, prior to or after their relationship with their current firm is terminated, shall not induce clients of their current firm to cancel exclusive contractual agreements between the client and that firm. This does not preclude REALTORS* (principals) from establishing agreements with their associated licensees governing assignability of exclusive agreements. *(Adopted 1/98, Amended 1/10)*

Article 17

In the event of contractual disputes or specific non-contractual disputes as defined in Standard of Practice 17-4 between REALTORS* (principals) associated with different firms, arising out of their relationship as REALTORS*, the REALTORS* shall submit the dispute to arbitration in accordance with the regulations of their Board or Boards rather than litigate the matter.

In the event clients of REALTORS* wish to arbitrate contractual disputes arising out of real estate transactions, REALTORS* shall arbitrate those disputes in accordance with the regulations of their Board, provided the clients agree to be bound by the decision.

The obligation to participate in arbitration contemplated by this Article includes the obligation of REALTORS* (principals) to cause their firms to arbitrate and be bound by any award. *(Amended 1/01)*

- **Standard of Practice 17-1**

  The filing of litigation and refusal to withdraw from it by REALTORS* in an arbitrable matter constitutes a refusal to arbitrate. *(Adopted 2/86)*

- **Standard of Practice 17-2**

  Article 17 does not require REALTORS* to arbitrate in those circumstances when all parties to the dispute advise the Board in writing that they choose not to arbitrate before the Board. *(Amended 1/93)*

- **Standard of Practice 17-3**

  REALTORS*, when acting solely as principals in a real estate transaction, are not obligated to arbitrate disputes with other REALTORS* absent a specific written agreement to the contrary. *(Adopted 1/96)*

• **Standard of Practice 17-4**

Specific non-contractual disputes that are subject to arbitration pursuant to Article 17 are:

1. Where a listing broker has compensated a cooperating broker and another cooperating broker subsequently claims to be the procuring cause of the sale or lease. In such cases the complainant may name the first cooperating broker as respondent and arbitration may proceed without the listing broker being named as a respondent. When arbitration occurs between two (or more) cooperating brokers and where the listing broker is not a party, the amount in dispute and the amount of any potential resulting award is limited to the amount paid to the respondent by the listing broker and any amount credited or paid to a party to the transaction at the direction of the respondent. Alternatively, if the complaint is brought against the listing broker, the listing broker may name the first cooperating broker as a third-party respondent. In either instance the decision of the hearing panel as to procuring cause shall be conclusive with respect to all current or subsequent claims of the parties for compensation arising out of the underlying cooperative transaction. (*Adopted 1/97, Amended 1/07*)

2. Where a buyer or tenant representative is compensated by the seller or landlord, and not by the listing broker, and the listing broker, as a result, reduces the commission owed by the seller or landlord and, subsequent to such actions, another cooperating broker claims to be the procuring cause of sale or lease. In such cases the complainant may name the first cooperating broker as respondent and arbitration may proceed without the listing broker being named as a respondent. When arbitration occurs between two (or more) cooperating brokers and where the listing broker is not a party, the amount in dispute and the amount of any potential resulting award is limited to the amount paid to the respondent by the seller or landlord and any amount credited

or paid to a party to the transaction at the direction of the respondent. Alternatively, if the complaint is brought against the listing broker, the listing broker may name the first cooperating broker as a third-party respondent. In either instance the decision of the hearing panel as to procuring cause shall be conclusive with respect to all current or subsequent claims of the parties for compensation arising out of the underlying cooperative transaction. *(Adopted 1/97, Amended 1/07)*

3. Where a buyer or tenant representative is compensated by the buyer or tenant and, as a result, the listing broker reduces the commission owed by the seller or landlord and, subsequent to such actions, another cooperating broker claims to be the procuring cause of sale or lease. In such cases the complainant may name the first cooperating broker as respondent and arbitration may proceed without the listing broker being named as a respondent. Alternatively, if the complaint is brought against the listing broker, the listing broker may name the first cooperating broker as a third-party respondent. In either instance the decision of the hearing panel as to procuring cause shall be conclusive with respect to all current or subsequent claims of the parties for compensation arising out of the underlying cooperative transaction. *(Adopted 1/97)*

4. Where two or more listing brokers claim entitlement to compensation pursuant to open listings with a seller or landlord who agrees to participate in arbitration (or who requests arbitration) and who agrees to be bound by the decision. In cases where one of the listing brokers has been compensated by the seller or landlord, the other listing broker, as complainant, may name the first listing broker as respondent and arbitration may proceed between the brokers. *(Adopted 1/97)*

5. Where a buyer or tenant representative is compensated by the seller or landlord, and not by the listing broker, and the listing broker, as a result, reduces the commission owed by the seller

or landlord and, subsequent to such actions, claims to be the procuring cause of sale or lease. In such cases arbitration shall be between the listing broker and the buyer or tenant representative and the amount in dispute is limited to the amount of the reduction of commission to which the listing broker agreed. *(Adopted 1/05)*

- **Standard of Practice 17-5**

  The obligation to arbitrate established in Article 17 includes disputes between REALTORS˚ (principals) in different states in instances where, absent an established inter-association arbitration agreement, the REALTOR˚ (principal) requesting arbitration agrees to submit to the jurisdiction of, travel to, participate in, and be bound by any resulting award rendered in arbitration conducted by the respondent(s) REALTOR˚'s association, in instances where the respondent(s) REALTOR˚'s association determines that an arbitrable issue exists. *(Adopted 1/07)*

The **Code of Ethics** *was adopted in 1913. Amended at the Annual Convention in 1924, 1928, 1950, 1951, 1952, 1955, 1956, 1961, 1962, 1974, 1982, 1986, 1987, 1989, 1990, 1991, 1992, 1993, 1994, 1995, 1996, 1997, 1998, 1999, 2000, 2001, 2002, 2003, 2004, 2005, 2006, 2007, 2008 and 2009.*

<u>Explanatory Notes</u>

The reader should be aware of the following policies which have been approved by the Board of Directors of the National Association:

In filing a charge of an alleged violation of the Code of Ethics by a REALTOR˚, the charge must read as an alleged violation of one or more Articles of the Code. Standards of Practice may be cited in support of the charge.

The Standards of Practice serve to clarify the ethical obligations imposed by the various Articles and supplement, and do not substitute for, the Case Interpretations in Interpretations of the Code of Ethics.

Modifications to existing Standards of Practice and additional new Standards of Practice are approved from time to time. Readers are cautioned to ensure that the most recent publications are utilized.

APPENDIX B

Home Affordable Modification Program Guidelines
March 4, 2009

Trial loan modifications consistent with these Guidelines may be offered to homeowners beginning on this date, March 4, 2009, and may be considered for acceptance into the Home Affordable Modification Program upon completion of the trial period and other conditions. These Guidelines, however, do not constitute a contract offer binding on the Department of the Treasury.

Program Elements Described in the Guidelines

Monthly Payment Reduction Cost Share:	Treasury will partner with financial institutions to reduce homeowners' monthly mortgage payments. The lender will have to first reduce payments on mortgages to no greater than 38% Front-End Debt-to-Income (DTI) ratio. Treasury will match further reductions in monthly payments dollar-for-dollar with the lender/investor, down to a 31% Front-End DTI ratio for the borrower.
Servicer Incentive Payments and Pay for Success Fees:	Servicers will receive an up-front Servicer Incentive Payment of $1,000 for each eligible modification meeting guidelines established under this initiative. Servicers will also receive Pay for Success payments—as long as the borrower stays in the program—of up to $1,000 each year for up to three years. Similar incentives will be paid for Hope for Homeowner refinances.

Borrower Pay-for-Performance Success Payments:	Borrowers are eligible to receive a Pay-for-Performance Success Payment that goes straight toward reducing the principal balance on the mortgage loan as long as the borrower is current on his or her monthly payments. Borrowers can receive up to $1,000 of Pay-for-Performance Success Payments each year for up to five years.
Current Borrower One-Time Bonus Incentive:	One-time bonus incentive payments of $1,500 to lender/ investors and $500 to servicers will be provided for modifications made while a borrower is still current on mortgage payments. The servicer will be required to maintain records and documentation evidencing that the Trial Period payment arrangements were agreed to while the borrower was less than 30 days delinquent. The servicer must comply with any express pooling and servicing contractual restrictions for modifying current loans.
Program Payment Conditions:	No payments under the program to the lender/ investor, servicer, or borrower will be made unless and until the servicer has entered into the program agreements with Treasury's financial agent. Servicers must enter into the program agreements with Treasury's financial agent no later than December 31, 2009.

Eligibility Requirements

Pooling and Servicing Agreements:	The program guidelines reflect usual and customary industry standards for mortgage loan modifications contained in typical servicing agreements, including pooling and servicing agreements (PSAs) governing private label securitizations. Participating servicers are required to consider all eligible loans under the program guidelines unless prohibited by the rules of the applicable PSA and/or other investor servicing agreements. Participating servicers are required to use reasonable efforts to remove any prohibitions and obtain waivers or approvals from all necessary parties.
Origination Date of Loan Subject to Modification:	The mortgage to be modified must have been originated on or before January 1, 2009.
Program Expiration:	New borrowers will be accepted until December 31, 2012. Program payments will be made for up to five years after the date of entry into a Home Affordable Modification. Monitoring will continue through the life of the program.

Qualification Terms:	• The home must be an owner occupied, single family 1–4 unit property (including condominium, cooperative, and manufactured home affixed to a foundation and treated as real property under state law).
	
	• The home must be a primary residence (verified with tax return, credit report, and other documentation such as a utility bill).
	
	• The home may not be investor-owned.
	
	• The home may not be vacant or condemned.
	
	• Borrowers in bankruptcy are not automatically eliminated from consideration for a modification.
	
	• Borrowers in active litigation regarding the mortgage loan can qualify for a modification without waiving their legal rights.
	
	    First lien loans must have an unpaid principal balance (prior to capitalization of arrearages) equal to or less than
	
	    o 1 Unit: $729,750
	
	    o 2 Units: $934,200
	
	    o 3 Units: $1,129,250
	
	    o 4 Units: $1,403,400

In Foreclosure Process:	Any foreclosure action will be temporarily suspended during the trial period, or while borrowers are considered for alternative foreclosure prevention options. In the event that the Home Affordable Modification or alternative foreclosure prevention options fail, the foreclosure action may be resumed.
Current LTV:	There is no minimum or maximum LTV ratio for eligibility purposes.
Loan Type Exclusions:	Loans can only be modified under the Home Affordable Modification program once.
Subordinate Financing:	Subordinate liens are not included in the Front-End DTI calculation, but they are included in the Back-End DTI calculation.
Solicitation to Borrowers/Incoming Inquiries:	Services should follow any existing express contractual restrictions with respect to solicitation or borrowers for modifications.

Underwriting Analysis

Front-End DTI Target:	Front-End DTI is the ratio of PITIA to Monthly Gross Income. PITIA is defined as principal, interest, taxes, insurance (including homeowners insurance and hazard and flood insurance) and homeowner's association and/or condominium fees. Mortgage insurance premiums are excluded from the PITIA calculation.
	The Front-End DTI Target is 31%. The Standard Waterfall step that results in a Front-End DTI closest to 31%, without going below 31%, will satisfy the Front-End DTI Target. There is no restriction on reducing Front-End DTI below 31%, but any portion of the reduction below 31% will not be covered by the Payment Reduction Cost Share.

Property Value:	The servicer may use, at its discretion, either one of the government sponsored enterprises (GSEs) automated valuation model (AVM)—provided that the AVM renders a reliable confidence score—or a broker price opinion (BPO).
	As an alternative, the servicer may rely on the AVM it uses internally provided that (i) the servicer's is subject to supervision by a Federal regulatory agency, (ii) the servicer's primary Federal regulatory agency has reviewed the model and/or its validation, and (iii) the AVM renders a reliable confidence score.
	If the GSE or servicer AVM is unable to render a value with a reliable confidence score, the servicer must obtain an assessment of the property value utilizing a property valuation method acceptable to the servicer's Federal regulatory agency, e.g., in accordance with the Interagency Appraisal and Evaluation Guidelines (as though such guidelines apply to loan modification), or a BPO.
	In all cases, the property valuation may not be more than 60 days old.
Income and Asset Validation:	The borrower's income will be verified by requiring a signed Form 4506-T (Request for Transcript of Tax Return) and obtaining the most recent tax return on file for each borrower on the note. For wage earners, the two most recent pay stubs for each wage earner on the note will also be required. For self-employed borrowers or for non-wage income, the borrower's income will be verified by obtaining other third-party documents that provide reasonably reliable evidence of income.
	Borrowers must also represent and warrant that they do not have sufficient liquid assets to make their monthly mortgage payments.

Monthly Gross Income:	The borrower's Monthly Gross Income is the amount before any payroll deductions includes wages and salaries, overtime pay, commissions, fees, tips, bonuses, housing allowances, other compensation for personal services, Social Security payments, including Social Security received by adults on behalf of minors or by minors intended for their own support, annuities, insurance policies, retirement funds, pensions, disability or death benefits, unemployment benefits, rental income and other income. Monthly net income can be used for preliminary screening and qualification. If used, the servicer will need to multiply net income by 1.25 to get an estimate of Monthly Gross Income.
Back-End DTI:	The Back-End DTI is the ratio of the borrower's total monthly debt payments (such as Front-End PITIA, any mortgage insurance premiums, payments on all installment debts, monthly payments on all junior liens, alimony, car lease payments, aggregate negative net rental income from all investment properties owned, and monthly mortgage payments for second homes) to the borrower's Monthly Gross Income. The servicer must validate monthly installment, revolving debt and secondary mortgage debt by pulling a credit report for each borrower or a joint report for a married couple. The servicer must also consider information obtained from the borrower orally or in writing concerning incremental monthly obligations.

	Borrowers who otherwise qualify for a modification under this program, but who would have a post-modification Back-End DTI greater than or equal to 55%, will be provided with a letter stating that they are required to work with a HUD-approved counselor and the modification will not take effect until they provide a signed statement indicating that they will obtain counseling.
Reasonably Foreseeable / Imminent Default:	Every potentially eligible borrower who calls or writes in to their servicer in reference to a modification must be screened for hardship. This screen must ascertain whether the borrower has had a change in circumstances that causes financial hardship, or is facing a recent or imminent increase in the payment that is likely to create a financial hardship (payment shock). If the borrower reports a material change in circumstances, the servicer must ask about current income and assets, and current expenses as well as the specific circumstances relating to the claimed financial hardship. Each of these elements shall be verified through documentation.
	If the servicer determines that a non-defaulted borrower facing a financial hardship is in Imminent Default and will be unable to make his or her mortgage payment in the immediate future, the servicer must apply the NPV test.

Required Modifications and Optional Modifications:	A standard NPV Test will be required on each loan that is in Imminent Default or is at least 60 days delinquent under the MBA delinquency calculation. This NPV Test will compare the net present value (NPV) of cash flows expected from a modification to the net present value of cash flows expected in the absence of modification. If the NPV of the modification scenario is greater, the NPV results are deemed positive. The NPV Test applies to the Standard Waterfall only and does not require consideration of principal forgiveness. However, the servicer may choose to forgive principal if the servicer determines that principal forgiveness improves the likelihood of loan performance and the value of modification. Required parameters for the NPV Test will be published separately. If the NPV Test generates a positive result when applying the Standard Waterfall, the servicer is required to offer a Home Affordable Modification to the borrower. If the NPV Test generates a negative result, modification is optional, unless prohibited under contract. The monthly payment reduction incentive is available for any Home Affordable Modification, whether or not NPV positive, that meets the eligibility requirements and is performed according to the waterfall described below. If the NPV Test result is negative and a Home Affordable Modification is not pursued, the lender/investor must seek other foreclosure prevention alternatives, including alternative modification programs, deed-in-lieu and short sale programs.

Loan Modification and Standard Waterfall

Overview:	Services will follow the Standard Waterfall described below to reduce monthly payments to the 31% Front-End DTI Target defined above. The initiative will reimburse lenders/investors for one-half of the cost of reducing monthly payments from a level consistent with a 38% Front End DTI Ratio (or less, if the unmodified DTI is less than 38%) down to a level consistent with a 31% Front-End DTI Ratio. This Payment Reduction Cost Share can last for up to five years.
Hope for Homeowners:	Servicers will be required to consider a borrower for refinancing into the Hope for Homeowners program when feasible. Servicer incentive payments will be paid for Hope for Homeowner refinances. If the underwriting process for a Hope for Homeowners refinance would delay eligible borrowers from receiving a modification offer, servicers will use the Standard Waterfall to begin the Home Affordability Modification and work to complete the Hope for Homeowners refinance during the Trial Modification Period. Consideration for a Hope for Homeowners refinance should not delay eligible borrowers from receiving a modification offer and beginning the Trial Modification Period.
Standard Waterfall Process:	Step 1a: Request Monthly Gross Income as specified above. Step 1b: Validate total first lien debt and monthly payments (PITIA). For purposes of making a provisional modification offer during the trial modification period, the borrower's unverified income and debt payments can be used. Provisional information and modification terms will be verified in a timely manner.

Step 2: Capitalize arrearage. Servicers may capitalize accrued interest, past due real estate taxes and insurance premiums, delinquency charges paid to third parties in the ordinary course of servicing and not retained by the servicer, any required escrow advances already paid by the servicer and any required escrow advances by the servicer that are currently due and will be paid by the servicer during the Trial Period. Late fees are not capitalized.

Step 3: Target a Front-End DTI of 31%. The lender/investor shall follow steps 4, 5, and 6 to reduce the borrower's payment to the level corresponding to the Front-End DTI Target.

Step 4: Reduce the interest rate to reach the Front-End DTI Target (subject to a floor of 2%). The note rate should be reduced in increments of 0.125%, and should bring the monthly payment as close as possible to the Front-End DTI Target without going below 31%. If the resulting modified interest rate is at or above the Interest Rate Cap, this modified interest rate will be the new note rate for the remaining loan term. If the resulting modified interest rate is below the Interest Rate Cap, this modified interest rate will be in effect for the first five years, followed by annual increases of 1% (100 basis points) per year or such lesser amount as may be needed until the interest rate reaches the Interest Rate Cap, at which time it will be fixed for the remaining loan term.

Step 5: If the Front-End DTI Target has not been reached, extend the term of the loan up to 40 years. If term extension is not permitted extend amortization. The 40-year term begins at the start of the modification (after the borrower successfully completes the Trial

	Period). Note that the servicer should only extend to a term that is necessary to reach the Front-End DTI Target; there is no requirement to extend to a 40-year term. Step 6: If the Front-End DTI Target has not been reached, forbear principal. If there is a principal forbearance amount, a balloon payment of that forbearance amount is due on the maturity date, upon sale of the property, or upon payoff of the interest bearing balance. If the modification does not pass the NPV Test and the servicer chooses to modify the loan, the modified balance must be no lower than the current property value.
Principal Reduction Option:	There is no requirement to use principal reduction under the Home Affordable Modification program; however, servicers may forgive principal to achieve the Front-End DTI Target. Principal forgiveness can be used on a standalone basis or before any step in the Standard Waterfall process. If principal forgiveness is used, subsequent steps in the Standard Waterfall may not be skipped. If principal is forgiven and the rate is not reduced, the rate will be frozen at its existing level and treated as a modified rate for the purposes of the Interest Rate Cap. In the event of principal forgiveness, the Payment Reduction Cost Share continues to be based on the change in the borrower's monthly payment from 38% to 31% Front-End DTI ratio and is limited to five years.

Modification Terms

Interest Rate Floor:	The Interest Rate Floor for modified loans is 2%.
Interest Rate Cap:	The modified interest rate must remain in place for five years, after which time the interest rate will be gradually increased 1% (100 basis points) per year or such lesser amount as may be needed until it reaches the Interest Rate Cap. The Interest Rate Cap for the modified loan is the lesser of (i) the fully indexed and fully amortizing original contractual rate or (ii) the Freddie Mac Primary Mortgage Market Survey rate for 30-year fixed rate conforming mortgage loans, rounded to the nearest 0.125%, as of the date that the modification document is prepared. If the modified rate exceeds the Freddie Mac Primary Mortgage Market Survey rate in effect on the date the modification document is prepared, the modified rate will be the new note rate for the remaining loan term.
Principal Forbearance:	No interest will accrue on the forbearance amount. If the option to forebear principal is selected, the servicer shall forbear on collecting the deferred portion of the Capitalized Balance until the earliest of (i) the maturity of the modified loan, (ii) a sale of the property, or (iii) a pay-off or refinancing of the loan.
Redefaulting Loans:	A loan will be considered to have redefaulted when the borrower reaches a 90-day delinquency status under the MBA delinquency calculation. Redefaulting Loans will be terminated from the program, and no further payments of any kind will be made to the lender/investor, servicer, or borrower. Redefaulting Loans should be considered for other loss mitigation programs prior to being referred to foreclosure.

Approval Conditions

Trial Period Required:	Successful completion of the trial modification period and entry into program agreements between the servicer and Treasury's financial agent are prerequisites for any payments to the lender/investor, servicer, or borrower. Modification is effective the first calendar month following the successful completion of the Trial Period. Successful completion means that the borrower is current (under the MBA delinquency calculation) at the end of the Trial Period. Borrowers in foreclosure restart states will be considered to have failed the Trial Period if they are not current at the time the foreclosure sale is scheduled. No payments under the program to the lender/investor, servicer, or borrower will be made during the Trial Period. No payments under the program to the lender/investor, servicer, or borrower will be made if the Trial Period is not completed successfully. No payments under the program to the lender /investor, servicer, or borrower will be made unless and until the servicer has entered into the program agreements with Treasury's financial agent.
Length of Trial Period:	The Trial Period will last 90 days (three payments at modified terms) or longer if necessary to comply with investor contractual obligations. The borrower must be current at the end of the Trial Period to obtain a Home Affordable Modification.

Escrows:	Services are required to escrow for modified borrowers' real estate taxes and mortgage-related insurance payments immediately if they have the capability of processing these payments or are already using a third-party vendor for this purpose. Servicers who do not have this capacity must implement an escrow process within six months of the program agreement.
Counseling Requirements:	For borrowers with a Back-End DTI of 55% or higher, the servicer must inform the borrower of the availability and advantages of counseling and provide a list of local HUD-approved counselors. The servicer must provide the borrower with a letter stating that counseling is a requirement of the modification terms. This letter may be required by counselors in order to begin counseling. The modification will not take effect until the borrower represents in writing that he or she will obtain counseling.
Assumable:	If the modified loan was assumable prior to modification, a Home Affordable Modification cancels this feature.

Fees/Charges

Modification Fees and Charges to Borrower:	There are no modification fees or charges borne by the borrower.
Modification Fees and Charges Reimbursable by Investor:	Modification fees and charges to the servicer will be reimbursable by the investor. These include notary fees, property valuation, and other required fees. Servicer reimbursement by the investor will take place within the normal process between the servicer and the investor.

Unpaid Late Fees Waived:	Unpaid late fees will be waived for the borrower. These include late fees prior to the start of the Trial Period and accrued during the period.
Credit Report:	The servicer will cover the cost of the credit report.
Servicer Compensation:	Compensation is provided to the servicer that performs the loss mitigation or modification activities. Upon modification following successful completion of the Trial Period, and contingent on signing the program servicer agreement, the servicer will receive an incentive fee of $1,000 for each eligible modification meeting Home Affordable Modification guidelines.

Servicers will also receive Pay for Success fees—payable 12 months from the effective date of the Trial Period as long as the borrower continues in the program—of up to $1,000 each year for three years. Servicers will no longer receive Pay for Success incentive payments for Redefaulting Loans or for loans that have paid off subject to certain *de minimis* constraints (discussed below). For loans modified while still current under the MBA delinquency calculation, the servicer will receive a Current Borrower One-Time Incentive of $500 following successful completion of the Trial Period.

Lenders that service their own loans are eligible for these incentives. Throughout this document the term "servicer" means the party that is responsible for performing the modification activities.

Similar incentives will be paid for Hope for Homeowner refinances. |

Borrower Cash Contribution:	The investor may not require the borrower to contribute cash.
Lender/Investor Compensation:	Lenders/investors will be compensated only in the event that the Front-End DTI Target or a lower Front-End DTI is achieved. Lender/investors will follow the Standard Waterfall specified above to reach a monthly payment that satisfies the Front-End DTI Target. As described above, Treasury will provide compensation based on one half of the dollar difference between the monthly payment for a 31% Front-End DTI Ratio and the lesser of (i) the monthly payment for a 38% Front-End DTI Ratio or (ii) the borrower's current monthly payment. This compensation will be provided for up to five years or until the loan is paid off. Upon a modification becoming effective following successful completion of the Trial Period by a borrower who was current prior to the start of the Trial Period, lenders/investors will be paid a $1,500 Current Borrower One-Time Incentive, subject to certain *de minimis* constraints (discussed below) No monthly lender/investor payments will be made during the Trial Period. Monthly lender/investor payments will begin after the Trial Period is successfully completed, the servicer signs a service agreement with Treasury, and formal modification begins. No monthly lender/investor payments will be made if the Trial Period is not completed successfully.

Borrower Compensation:	Borrowers will be eligible to accrue up to $1,000 each year in Pay-for-Performance Success Payments for up to five years, a total of up to $5,000 over five years, subject to certain *de minimis* constraints (discussed below). Accruals are based on on-time payment performance. The first annual principal balance reduction will be effective 12 months after entering the Trial Period as long as the borrower is not terminated from the program. In any given month, the borrower's mortgage payment must be made on time, accounting for standard servicer grace periods, in order to accrue the monthly Pay for Performance Success Payment. The borrower will receive information on a monthly basis regarding the accrual of these payments.
	The payment will be directed to the servicer, who will reduce the principal balance by the payment amount (but not by more than $1,000 per year) for five years if the borrower continues in the program. Payments are to be applied directly and entirely to reduce the principal balance, and any applicable prepayment penalties on partial principal prepayment made by the government must be waived. The equivalent of three months of Pay-for-Performance Success Payments will be made upon successful completion of the Trial Period, contingent upon the servicer signing a service agreement with the Treasury.
	Borrowers who are terminated from the program lose their right to outstanding accruals.

De Minimis Constraint:	To qualify for servicer Pay for Success payments and borrower Pay for Performance Success Payments, the modification must reduce the monthly payment by a minimum of 6%. The monthly payment is the PITIA payment, as used in defining DTI, with the loan fully indexed and fully amortized.
	When paid, servicer annual Pay for Success payments and borrower Pay for Performance Success Payments will be the lesser of (i) $1,000 or (ii) half the reduction in the borrower's annualized monthly payment.
	The *de minimis* constraint does not apply to the up-front Servicer Incentive Payment, the Payment Reduction Cost Share, or the Home Price Depreciation Reserve Payment.

Consumer Protection

Disclosure:	When promoting or describing loan modifications, servicers should provide borrowers with information designed to help them understand the modification terms that are being offered and the modification process. Servicers also must provide borrowers with clear and understandable written information about the material terms, costs, and risks of the modified mortgage loan in a timely manner to enable borrowers to make informed decisions.

Fair Lending:	Servicers' modifications under this program must comply with the Equal Credit Opportunity Act and the Fair Housing Act, which prohibit discrimination on a prohibited basis in connection with mortgage transactions. Loan modification programs are subject to the fair lending laws, and servicers and lenders should ensure that they do not treat a borrower less favorably than other borrowers on grounds such as race, religion, national origin, sex, marital or family status, age, handicap, or receipt of public assistance income in connection with any loan modification. These laws also prohibit redlining.
Consumer Inquiries and Complaints:	Servicers should have procedures and systems in place to be able to respond to inquiries and complaints relating to loan modifications. Servicers should ensure that such inquiries and complaints are provided fair consideration, and timely and appropriate responses and resolution.

Monitoring

Documentation:	Servicers will be required to maintain records of key data points for verification/compliance reviews. These documents may include, but are not limited to, borrower eligibility and qualification, underwriting criteria, and incentive payments. These documents also include a hardship affidavit, which every borrower is required to execute. Borrowers will be required to provide declarations under penalty of perjury attesting to the truth of the information that they have provided to the servicer to allow the servicer to determine the borrower's eligibility for entry into the Home Affordable Modification Program. Detailed guidance on data requirements will be released separately.
Anti-Fraud Measures:	Measures to prevent and detect fraud, such as documentation and audit requirements, will be described in the servicer guidelines and the program guidelines in the financial agency agreements with Fannie Mae and Freddie Mac. Additional fraud protection measures will be announced by Treasury. Participating servicers and lenders/investors are not required to modify the loan if there is reasonable evidence indicating the borrower submitted false or misleading information or otherwise engaged in fraud in connection with the modification. Servicers should employ reasonable policies and/or procedures to identify fraud in the modification process.

Data Collection:	Servicers will be required to collect and transmit borrower and property data in order to ensure compliance with the program as well as to measure its effectiveness. Data elements may include data needed to perform underwriting analysis, loan modification and waterfall analysis, and modification terms. In addition, borrower profiles and property level information may be included. Detailed guidance on data requirements will be released separately.
Accounting and Legal:	The provisions of the Program should not be construed to override, void or in any way modify the responsibility of the management of lenders and servicers for preparing financial statements and regulatory reports in accordance with all applicable generally accepted accounting principles, including standards such as Statement of Financial Accounting Standards (SFAS) No. 15, *Accounting by Debtors and Creditors for Troubled Debt Restructurings*, SFAS No. 114, *Accounting by Creditors for Impairment of a Loan*, SFAS No. 133, *Accounting for Derivative Instruments and Hedging Activities*, SFAS No. 140, *Accounting for Transfers and Servicing of Financial Assets and Extinguishments of Liabilities*, and AICPA Statement of Position 03-3, *Accounting for Certain Loans or Debt Securities Acquired in a Transfer*, and their related amendments and interpretations.

Other Program Features

Home Price Depreciation Payments:	To encourage lenders/investors to modify more mortgages, compensation will be provided to partially offset probable losses from home price declines. This will be structured as a simple cash payment on each modified loan while the loan remains active in the program.
Payments for Short Sales and Deeds-in-Lieu:	Compensation will be provided to servicers and borrowers in order to facilitate short sales or deeds-in-lieu in those cases in which borrowers either fail the net present value (NPV) test (described below) or fail to qualify for, or default under, the modification program.
Second Lien Elimination Payments:	To reduce the borrower's overall indebtedness and improve loan performance, additional incentives will be provided to extinguish junior liens on homes with first-lien loans that are modified under the program.
Government Loan Programs:	FHA, VA, and rural housing loans will be addressed through standalone modification programs run by those agencies. FHA's Hope for Homeowners refinancing program will also be included in a parallel incentive program.

Net Present Value Model Parameters

NPV Test:	An NPV Test will be required on each loan that is Imminent Default or is at least 60 days delinquent under the MBA delinquency calculation. This NPV test will compare the net present value (NPV) of cash flows expected from a modification to the net present value of cash flows expected in the absence of modification. If the NPV of the modification scenario is greater, the NPV result is deemed positive, and the servicer must modify the loan (absent fraud, etc.). However, an "NPV positive" result is not necessary to qualify a loan for a Home Affordable Modification and the associated lender/ investor, servicer, and borrower payments.
Standard NPV Model:	To provide a consistent and industry-wide approach to the required NPV Tests, Treasury will set forth a Standard NPV Model with parameters specified below. Complete details on each component outlined below are forthcoming.
Discount Rate:	The program allows the servicer to choose the Discount Rate to use in the NPV Model, subject to a program-determined ceiling that will be sensitive to the market-determined cost of funds. The ceiling on the allowable Discount Rate for the NPV Test is the Freddie Mac Primary Mortgage Market Survey rate (PMMS), plus a spread of 2.5 percentage points. The PMMS is the conventional mortgage rate published in the Federal Reserve's H.15 bulletin.

	The servicer may choose a different Discount Rate for loans in portfolio versus loans in investor pools, but may not otherwise apply different rates to different loans in the servicing book. For example, it may choose to use a Discount Rate equal to the PMMS + 2.0 percent for its investor pools and a Discount Rate equal to the PMMS for its loans in portfolio.
Cure Rate and Redefault Rate:	The Cure Rates and Redefault Rates will be obtained from a default equation with parameters based on GSE analytics and program portfolio data except where servicers use custom parameters (see below). Treasury, in consultation with an inter-agency team of government officials, will update these tables periodically based on income data.
Property Value:	Property value will be determined in accordance with the Guidelines.
Incentive Payments:	Incentive payments, including the Payment Reduction Cost Share, annual borrower performance bonus payments toward principal, and Current Borrower One-Time Bonus Incentive, will be determined in accordance with the Guidelines.
Other Parameters:	The remaining parameters will come from data sets held or produced by the Federal Housing Finance Agency: home price forecast, valuation of the house price depreciation reserve, foreclosure timelines, and foreclosure cost and REO stigma.

NPV Test Customization:	Servicers having at least a $40 billion servicing book will have an option to substitute a set of Cure Rates and Redefault Rates estimated based on the experience of their own aggregate portfolios. A servicer using this option should take into account, as feasible, current LTV, current DTI, current credit score, delinquency status, and other relevant variables the servicer identifies.
	The Cure and Redefault Rates must be empirically validated where possible. Servicer judgment regarding the effect of DTI is expected, given the limited data available and the likelihood that the new program will materially affect Cure and Redefault Rates. However, all assumptions must be tested as program data become available and revised as appropriate.
	A servicer who chooses to use customized Cure and Redefault Rates must apply the same assumptions for Cure and Redefault Rate to the entire servicing portfolio, without distinguishing between loans in portfolio and investor pools.
	Models and assumptions will be subject to review by federal bank supervisory agencies where applicable, and in all cases by Freddie Mac as program compliance agent.
	A servicer not meeting the size threshold may apply for permission to apply Cure Rates and Redefault Rates estimated based on the servicer's portfolio experience.

Mortgage Insurance:	For loans that have mortgage insurance (MI) coverage, the NPV Test will incorporate the value of the contingent claim payment in the event of default when evaluating projected foreclosure or modification scenarios. If the modification does not pass the NPV Test, then it will be referred to the appropriate MI company. The major MI companies have agreed to develop a mechanism by which they will pay partial claims where they deem appropriate to avoid foreclosure.

Source: Information provided by the U. S. Department of the Treasury

GLOSSARY

A

"A" Loan or "A" Paper: a credit rating where the FICO score is 660 or above. There have been no late mortgage payments within a 12-month period. This is the best credit rating to have when entering into a new loan.

ARM: Adjustable Rate Mortgage; a mortgage loan subject to changes in interest rates; when rates change, ARM monthly payments increase or decrease at intervals determined by the lender; the change in monthly payment amount, however, is usually subject to a cap.

Abstract of Title: documents recording the ownership of property throughout time.

Acceleration: the right of the lender to demand payment on the outstanding balance of a loan.

Acceptance: the written approval of the buyer's offer by the seller.

Additional Principal Payment: money paid to the lender in addition to the established payment amount used directly against the loan principal to shorten the length of the loan.

Adjustable-Rate Mortgage (ARM): a mortgage loan that does not have a fixed interest rate. During the life of the loan the interest rate will change based on the index rate. Also referred to as adjustable mortgage loans (AMLs) or variable-rate mortgages (VRMs).

Adjustment Date: the actual date that the interest rate is changed for an ARM.

Adjustment Index: the published market index used to calculate the interest rate of an ARM at the time of origination or adjustment.

Adjustment Interval: the time between the interest rate change and the monthly payment for an ARM. The interval is usually every one, three or five years depending on the index.

Affidavit: a signed, sworn statement made by the buyer or seller regarding the truth of information provided.

Amenity: a feature of the home or property that serves as a benefit to the buyer but that is not necessary to its use; may be natural (like location, woods, water) or man-made (like a swimming pool or garden).

American Society of Home Inspectors: the American Society of Home Inspectors is a professional association of independent home inspectors. Phone: (800) 743-2744

Amortization: a payment plan that enables you to reduce your debt gradually through monthly payments. The payments may be principal and interest, or interest-only. The monthly amount is based on the schedule for the entire term or length of the loan.

Annual Mortgagor Statement: yearly statement to borrowers detailing the remaining principal and amounts paid for taxes and interest.

Annual Percentage Rate (APR): a measure of the cost of credit, expressed as a yearly rate. It includes interest as well as other charges. Because all lenders, by federal law, follow the same rules to ensure the accuracy of the annual percentage rate, it provides consumers with a good basis for comparing the cost of loans, including mortgage plans. APR is a higher rate than the simple interest of the mortgage.

Application: the first step in the official loan approval process; this form is used to record important information about the potential borrower necessary to the underwriting process.

Application Fee: a fee charged by lenders to process a loan application.

Appraisal: a document from a professional that gives an estimate of a property's fair market value based on the sales of comparable homes in the area and the features of a property; an appraisal is generally required by a lender before loan approval to ensure that the mortgage loan amount is not more than the value of the property.

Appraisal Fee: fee charged by an appraiser to estimate the market value of a property.

Appraised Value: an estimation of the current market value of a property.

Appraiser: a qualified individual who uses his or her experience and knowledge to prepare the appraisal estimate.

Appreciation: an increase in property value.

Arbitration: a legal method of resolving a dispute without going to court.

As-is Condition: the purchase or sale of a property in its existing condition without repairs.

Asking Price: a seller's stated price for a property.

Assessed Value: the value that a public official has placed on any asset (used to determine taxes).

Assessments: the method of placing value on an asset for taxation purposes.

Assessor: a government official who is responsible for determining the value of a property for the purpose of taxation.

Assets: any item with measurable value.

Assumable Mortgage: when a home is sold, the seller may be able to transfer the mortgage to the new buyer. This means the mortgage is assumable. Lenders generally require a credit review of the new borrower and may charge a fee for the assumption. Some mortgages contain a due-on-sale clause, which means that the mortgage may not be transferable to a new buyer. Instead, the lender may make you pay the entire balance that is due when you sell the home. An assumable mortgage can help you attract buyers if you sell your home.

Assumption Clause: a provision in the terms of a loan that allows the buyer to take legal responsibility for the mortgage from the seller.

Automated Underwriting: loan processing completed through a computer-based system that evaluates past credit history to determine if a loan should be approved. This system removes the possibility of personal bias against the buyer.

B

"B" Loan or "B" Paper: FICO scores from 620–659. Factors include two 30-day late mortgage payments and two to three 30-day late installment loan payments in the last 12 months. No delinquencies over 60 days are allowed. Should be two to four years since a bankruptcy. Also referred to as Sub-Prime.

Back End Ratio (debt ratio): a ratio that compares the total of all monthly debt payments (mortgage, real estate taxes and insurance, car loans, and other consumer loans) to gross monthly income.

Back to Back Escrow: arrangements that an owner makes to oversee the sale of one property and the purchase of another at the same time.

Back-up Offer: an offer that is accepted by the Seller and placed in second position behind the first accepted offer.

Balance Sheet: a financial statement that shows the assets, liabilities, and net worth of an individual or company.

Balloon Loan or Mortgage: a mortgage that typically offers low rates for an initial period of time (usually 5, 7, or 10) years; after that time period elapses, the balance is due or is refinanced by the borrower.

Balloon Payment: the final lump sum payment due at the end of a balloon mortgage.

Bankruptcy: a federal law whereby a person's assets are turned over to a trustee and used to pay off outstanding debts; this usually occurs when someone owes more than they have the ability to repay.

Biweekly Payment Mortgage: a mortgage paid twice a month instead of once a month, reducing the amount of interest to be paid on the loan.

Borrower: a person who has been approved to receive a loan and is then obligated to repay it and any additional fees according to the loan terms.

Bridge Loan: a short-term loan paid back relatively fast. Normally used until a long-term loan can be processed.

Broker: a licensed individual or firm that charges a fee to serve as the mediator between the buyer and seller. Mortgage brokers are individuals in the business of arranging funding or negotiating contracts for a client, but who does not loan the money. A real estate broker is someone who helps find a house.

Broker's Price Opinion (BPO): a Broker's written opinion of the current market value of a property. This is usually done for lenders prior to foreclosure on a property.

Building Code: based on agreed upon safety standards within a specific area, a building code is a regulation that determines the design, construction, and materials used in building.

Budget: a detailed record of all income earned and spent during a specific period of time.

Buy Down: the seller pays an amount to the lender so the lender provides a lower rate and lower payments many times for an ARM. The seller may increase the sales price to cover the cost of the buy down.

C

"C" Loan or "C" Paper: FICO scores typically from 580–619. Factors include three to four 30-day late mortgage payments and four to six 30-day late installment loan payments or two to four 60-day late payments. Should be one to two years since bankruptcy. Also referred to as Sub-Prime.

Callable Debt: a debt security whose issuer has the right to redeem the security at a specified price on or after a specified date, but prior to its stated final maturity.

Cap: a limit, such as one placed on an adjustable rate mortgage, on how much a monthly payment or interest rate can increase or decrease, either at each adjustment period or during the life of the mortgage. Payment caps do not limit the amount of interest the lender is earning, so they may cause negative amortization.

Capacity: The ability to make mortgage payments on time, dependant on assets and the amount of income each month after paying housing costs, debts and other obligations.

Capital Gain: the profit received based on the difference of the original purchase price and the total sale price.

Capital Improvements: property improvements that either will enhance the property value or will increase the useful life of the property.

Capital or Cash Reserves: an individual's savings, investments, or assets.

Cash-Out Refinance: when a borrower refinances a mortgage at a higher principal amount to get additional money. Usually this occurs when the property has appreciated in value. For example, if a home has a current value of $100,000 and an outstanding mortgage of $60,000, the owner could refinance $80,000 and have additional $20,000 in cash.

Cash Reserves: a cash amount sometimes required of the buyer to be held in reserve in addition to the down payment and closing costs; the amount is determined by the lender.

Casualty Protection: property insurance that covers any damage to the home and personal property either inside or outside the home.

Certificate of Title: a document provided by a qualified source, such as a title company, that shows the property legally belongs to the current owner; before the title is transferred at closing, it should be clear and free of all liens or other claims.

Chapter 7 Bankruptcy: a bankruptcy that requires assets be liquidated in exchange for the cancellation of debt.

Chapter 13 Bankruptcy: this type of bankruptcy sets a payment plan between the borrower and the creditor monitored by the court. The homeowner can keep the property, but must make payments according to the court's terms within a 3 to 5 year period.

Charge-Off: the portion of principal and interest due on a loan that is written off when deemed to be uncollectible.

Clear Title: a property title that has no defects. Properties with clear titles are marketable for sale.

Closing: the final step in property purchase where the title is transferred from the seller to the buyer. Closing occurs at a meeting between the buyer, seller, settlement agent, and other agents. At the closing the seller receives payment for the property. Also known as settlement.

Closing Costs: fees for final property transfer not included in the price of the property. Typical closing costs include charges for the mortgage loan such as origination fees, discount points, appraisal fee, survey, title insurance, legal fees, real estate professional fees, prepayment of taxes and insurance, and real estate transfer taxes. A common estimate of a Buyer's closing costs is 2 to 4 percent of the purchase price of the home. A common estimate for Seller's closing costs is 3 to 9 percent.

Cloud On The Title: any condition which affects the clear title to real property.

Co-Borrower: an additional person that is responsible for loan repayment and is listed on the title.

Co-Signed Account: an account signed by someone in addition to the primary borrower, making both people responsible for the amount borrowed.

Co-Signer: a person that signs a credit application with another person, agreeing to be equally responsible for the repayment of the loan.

Collateral: security in the form of money or property pledged for the payment of a loan. For example, on a home loan, the home is the collateral and can be taken away from the borrower if mortgage payments are not made.

Collection Account: an unpaid debt referred to a collection agency to collect on the bad debt. This type of account is reported to the credit bureau and will show on the borrower's credit report.

Commission: an amount, usually a percentage of the property sales price that is collected by a real estate professional as a fee for negotiating the transaction. Traditionally the home seller pays the commission.

Common Stock: a security that provides voting rights in a corporation and pays a dividend after preferred stock holders have been paid. This is the most common stock held within a company.

Comparative Market Analysis (CMA): a property evaluation that determines property value by comparing similar properties sold within the last year.

Compensating Factors: factors that show the ability to repay a loan based on less traditional criteria, such as employment, rent, and utility payment history.

Condominium: a form of ownership in which individuals purchase and own a unit of housing in a multi-unit complex. The owner also shares financial responsibility for common areas.

Conforming Loan: is a loan that does not exceed Fannie Mae's and Freddie Mac's loan limits. Freddie Mac and Fannie Mae loans are referred to as conforming loans.

Consideration: an item of value given in exchange for a promise or act.

Construction Loan: a short-term, to finance the cost of building a new home. The lender pays the builder based on milestones accomplished during the building process. For example, once a sub-contractor pours the foundation and it is approved by inspectors the lender will pay for their service.

Contingency: a clause in a purchase contract outlining conditions that must be fulfilled before the contract is executed. Both, buyer or seller may include contingencies in a contract, but both parties must accept the contingency.

Conventional Loan: a private-sector loan, one that is not guaranteed or insured by the U.S. government.

Conversion Clause: a provision in some ARMs allowing it to change to a fixed-rate loan at some point during the term. Usually conversions are allowed at the end of the first adjustment period. At the time of the conversion, the new fixed rate is generally set at one of the rates then prevailing for fixed rate mortgages. There may be additional cost for this clause.

Convertible ARM: an adjustable-rate mortgage that provides the borrower the ability to convert to a fixed-rate within a specified time.

Cooperative (Co-op): residents purchase stock in a cooperative corporation that owns a structure; each stockholder is then entitled to live in a specific unit of the structure and is responsible for paying a portion of the loan.

Cost of Funds Index (COFI): an index used to determine interest rate changes for some adjustable-rate mortgages.

Counter Offer: a rejection to all or part of a purchase offer that negotiates different terms to reach an acceptable sales contract.

Covenants: legally enforceable terms that govern the use of property. These terms are transferred with the property deed. Discriminatory covenants are illegal and unenforceable. Also known as a condition, restriction, deed restriction, or restrictive covenant.

Credit: an agreement that a person will borrow money and repay it to the lender over time.

Credit Bureau: an agency that provides financial information and payment history to lenders about potential borrowers. Also known as a National Credit Repository.

Credit Counseling: education on how to improve bad credit and how to avoid having more debt than can be repaid.

Credit Enhancement: a method used by a lender to reduce default of a loan by requiring collateral, mortgage insurance, or other agreements.

Credit Grantor: the lender that provides a loan or credit.

Credit History: a record of an individual that lists all debts and the payment history for each. The report that is generated from the history is called a credit report. Lenders use this information to gauge a potential borrower's ability to repay a loan.

Credit Loss Ratio: the ratio of credit-related losses to the dollar amount of MBS outstanding and total mortgages owned by the corporation.

Credit Related Expenses: foreclosed property expenses plus the provision for losses.

Credit Related Losses: foreclosed property expenses combined with charge-offs.

Credit Repair Companies: Private, for-profit businesses that claim to offer consumers credit and debt repayment difficulties assistance with their credit problems and a bad credit report.

Credit Report: a report generated by the credit bureau that contains the borrower's credit history for the past seven years. Lenders use this information to determine if a loan will be granted.

Credit Risk: a term used to describe the possibility of default on a loan by a borrower.

Credit Score: a score calculated by using a person's credit report to determine the likelihood of a loan being repaid on time. Scores range from about 300–850: a lower score meaning a person is a higher risk, while a higher score means that there is less risk.

Credit Union: a non-profit financial institution federally regulated and owned by the members or people who use their services. Credit unions serve groups that hold a common interest and you have to become a member to use the available services.

Creditor: the lending institution providing a loan or credit.

Creditworthiness: the way a lender measures the ability of a person to qualify and repay a loan.

D

Debtor: The person or entity that borrows money. The term debtor may be used interchangeably with the term borrower.

Debt-to-Income Ratio: a comparison or ratio of gross income to housing and non-housing expenses. With the FHA, the monthly mortgage payment should be no more than 29% of monthly gross income (before taxes) and the mortgage payment combined with non-housing debts should not exceed 41% of income.

Debt Security: a security that represents a loan from an investor to an issuer. The issuer in turn agrees to pay interest in addition to the principal amount borrowed.

Deductible: the amount of cash payment that is made by the insured (the homeowner) to cover a portion of a damage or loss. Sometimes also called "out-of-pocket expenses." For example, out of a total damage claim of $1,000, the homeowner might pay a $250 deductible toward the loss, while the insurance company pays $750 toward the loss. Typically, the higher the deductible, the lower the cost of the policy.

Deed: a document that legally transfers ownership of property from one person to another. The deed is recorded on public record with the property description and the owner's signature. Also known as the title.

Deed-in-Lieu: to avoid foreclosure ("in lieu" of foreclosure), a deed is given to the lender to fulfill the obligation to repay the debt; this process does not allow the borrower to remain in the house but helps avoid the costs, time, and effort associated with foreclosure.

Default: the inability to make timely monthly mortgage payments or otherwise comply with mortgage terms. A loan is considered in default when payment has not been paid after 60 to 90 days. Once in default the lender can exercise legal rights defined in the contract to begin foreclosure proceedings

Delinquency: failure of a borrower to make timely mortgage payments under a loan agreement. Generally after 15 days a late fee may be assessed.

Deposit (Earnest Money): money put down by a potential buyer to show that they are serious about purchasing the home; it becomes part of the down payment if the offer is accepted, is returned if the offer is rejected, or is forfeited if the buyer pulls out of the deal. During the contingency period the money may be returned to the buyer if the contingencies are not met to the buyer's satisfaction.

Depreciation: a decrease in the value or price of a property due to changes in market conditions, wear and tear on the property, or other factors.

Derivative: a contract between two or more parties where the security is dependent on the price of another investment.

Disclosures: the release of relevant information about a property that may influence the final sale, especially if it represents defects or problems. "Full disclosure" usually refers to the responsibility of the seller to voluntarily provide all known information about the property. Some disclosures may be required by law, such as the federal requirement to warn of potential lead-based paint hazards in pre-1978 housing. A seller found to have knowingly lied about a defect may face legal penalties.

Discount Point: normally paid at closing and generally calculated to be equivalent to 1% of the total loan amount, discount points are paid to reduce the interest rate on a loan. In an ARM with an initial rate discount, the lender gives up a number of percentage points in interest to give you a lower rate and lower payments for part of the mortgage term (usually for one year or less). After the discount period, the ARM rate will probably go up depending on the index rate.

Down Payment: the portion of a home's purchase price that is paid in cash and is not part of the mortgage loan. This amount varies based on the loan type, but is determined by taking the difference of the sale price and the actual mortgage loan amount. Mortgage insurance is required when a down payment less than 20 percent is made.

Document Recording: after closing on a loan, certain documents are filed and made public record. Discharges for the prior mortgage holder are filed first. Then the deed is filed with the new owner's and mortgage company's names.

Due on Sale Clause: a provision of a loan allowing the lender to demand full repayment of the loan if the property is sold.

Duration: the number of years it will take to receive the present value of all future payments on a security to include both principal and interest.

E

Earnest Money (Deposit): money put down by a potential buyer to show that they are serious about purchasing the home; it becomes part of the down payment if the offer is accepted, is returned if the offer is rejected, or is forfeited if the buyer pulls out of the deal. During the contingency period the money may be returned to the buyer if the contingencies are not met to the buyer's satisfaction.

Earnings Per Share (EPS): a corporation's profit that is divided among each share of common stock. It is determined by taking the net earnings divided by the number of outstanding common stocks held. This is a way that a company reports profitability.

Easements: the legal rights that give someone other than the owner access to use property for a specific purpose. Easements may affect property values and are sometimes a part of the deed.

EEM: Energy Efficient Mortgage; an FHA program that helps homebuyers save money on utility bills by enabling them to finance the cost of adding energy efficiency features to a new or existing home as part of the home purchase

Eminent Domain: when a government takes private property for public use. The owner receives payment for its fair market value. The property can then proceed to condemnation proceedings.

Encroachments: a structure that extends over the legal property line on to another individual's property. The property surveyor will note any encroachment on the lot survey done before property transfer. The person who owns the structure will be asked to remove it to prevent future problems.

Encumbrance: anything that affects title to a property, such as loans, leases, easements, or restrictions.

Equal Credit Opportunity Act (ECOA): a federal law requiring lenders to make credit available equally without discrimination based on race, color, religion, national origin, age, sex, marital status, or receipt of income from public assistance programs.

Equity: an owner's financial interest in a property; calculated by subtracting the amount still owed on the mortgage loan(s) from the fair market value of the property.

Escape Clause: a provision in a purchase contract that allows either party to cancel part or the entire contract if the other does not respond to changes to the sale within a set period. The most common use of the escape clause is if the buyer makes the purchase offer contingent on the sale of another house.

Escrow: funds held in an account to be used by the lender to pay for home insurance and property taxes. The funds may also be held by a third party until contractual conditions are met and then paid out.

Escrow Account/Impound Account: a separate account into which the lender puts a portion of each monthly mortgage payment; an escrow account provides the funds needed for such expenses as property taxes, homeowners insurance, mortgage insurance, etc.

Estate: the ownership interest of a person in real property. The sum total of all property, real and personal, owned by a person.

Exclusive Listing: a written contract giving a real estate agent the exclusive right to sell a property for a specific timeframe.

F

FICO Score: FICO is an abbreviation for Fair Isaac Corporation and refers to a person's credit score based on credit history. Lenders and credit card companies use the number to decide if the person is likely to pay his or her bills. A credit score is evaluated using information from the three major credit bureaus and is usually between 300 and 850.

FSBO (For Sale by Owner): a home that is offered for sale by the owner without the benefit of a real estate professional.

Fair Credit Reporting Act: federal act to ensure that credit bureaus are fair and accurate protecting the individual's privacy rights enacted in 1971 and revised in October 1997.

Fair Housing Act: a law that prohibits discrimination in all facets of the home buying process on the basis of race, color, national origin, religion, sex, familial status, or disability.

Fair Market Value: the hypothetical price that a willing buyer and seller will agree upon when they are acting freely, carefully, and with complete knowledge of the situation.

Familial Status: HUD uses this term to describe a single person, a pregnant woman or a household with children under 18 living with parents or legal custodians who might experience housing discrimination.

Fannie Mae: Federal National Mortgage Association (FNMA); a federally chartered enterprise owned by private stockholders that purchases residential mortgages and converts them into securities for sale to investors; by purchasing mortgages, Fannie Mae supplies funds that lenders may loan to potential homebuyers. Also known as a Government Sponsored Enterprise (GSE).

FHA: Federal Housing Administration; established in 1934 to advance homeownership opportunities for all Americans; assists homebuyers by providing mortgage insurance to lenders to cover most losses that may occur when a borrower defaults; this encourages lenders to make loans to borrowers who might not qualify for conventional mortgages.

First Mortgage: the mortgage with first priority if the loan is not paid.

Fixed Expenses: payments that do not vary from month to month.

Fixed-Rate Mortgage: a mortgage with payments that remain the same throughout the life of the loan because the interest rate and other terms are fixed and do not change.

Fixture: personal property permanently attached to real estate or real property that becomes a part of the real estate.

Float: the act of allowing an interest rate and discount points to fluctuate with changes in the market.

Flood Insurance: insurance that protects homeowners against losses from a flood; if a home is located in a flood plain, the lender will require flood insurance before approving a loan.

Forbearance: a lender may decide not to take legal action when a borrower is late in making a payment. Usually this occurs when a borrower sets up a plan that both sides agree will bring overdue mortgage payments up to date.

Foreclosure: a legal process in which mortgaged property is sold to pay the loan of the defaulting borrower. Foreclosure laws are based on the statutes of each state.

Freddie Mac: Federal Home Loan Mortgage Corporation (FHLM); a federally chartered corporation that purchases residential mortgages, securitizes them, and sells them to investors; this provides lenders with funds for new homebuyers. Also known as a Government Sponsored Enterprise (GSE).

Front End Ratio: a percentage comparing a borrower's total monthly cost to buy a house (mortgage principal and interest, insurance, and real estate taxes) to monthly income before deductions.

G

GSE: abbreviation for Government Sponsored Enterprises: a collection of financial services corporations formed by the United States Congress to reduce interest rates for farmers and homeowners. Examples include Fannie Mae and Freddie Mac.

Ginnie Mae: Government National Mortgage Association (GNMA); a government-owned corporation overseen by the U.S. Department of Housing and Urban Development, Ginnie Mae pools FHA-insured and VA-guaranteed loans to back securities for private investment; as With Fannie Mae and Freddie Mac, the investment income provides funding that may then be lent to eligible borrowers by lenders.

Global Debt Facility: designed to allow investors all over the world to purchase debt (loans) of U.S. dollar and foreign currency through a variety of clearing systems.

Good Faith Estimate: an estimate of all closing fees including pre-paid and escrow items as well as lender charges; must be given to the borrower within three days after submission of a loan application.

Graduated Payment Mortgages: mortgages that begin with lower monthly payments that get slowly larger over a period of years, eventually reaching a fixed level and remaining there for the life of the loan. Graduated payment loans may be good if you expect your annual income to increase.

Grantee: an individual to whom an interest in real property is conveyed.

Grantor: an individual conveying an interest in real property.

Gross Income: money earned before taxes and other deductions. Sometimes it may include income from self-employment, rental property, alimony, child support, public assistance payments, and retirement benefits.

Guaranty Fee: payment to FannieMae from a lender for the assurance of timely principal and interest payments to MBS (Mortgage Backed Security) security holders.

H

HECM (Reverse Mortgage): the reverse mortgage is used by senior homeowners age 62 and older to convert the equity in their home into monthly streams of income and/or a line of credit to be repaid when they no longer occupy the home. A lending institution such as a mortgage lender, bank, credit union or savings and loan association funds the FHA insured loan, commonly known as HECM.

Hazard Insurance: protection against a specific loss, such as fire, wind, etc., over a period of time that is secured by the payment of a regularly scheduled premium.

HELP: Homebuyer Education Learning Program; an educational program from the FHA that counsels people about the home buying process; HELP covers topics like budgeting, finding a home, getting a loan, and home maintenance; in most cases, completion of the program may entitle the homebuyer to a reduced initial FHA mortgage insurance premium—from 2.25% to 1.75% of the home purchase price.

Home Equity Line of Credit: a mortgage loan, usually in second mortgage, allowing a borrower to obtain cash against the equity of a home, up to a predetermined amount.

Home Equity Loan: a loan backed by the value of a home (real estate). If the borrower defaults or does not pay the loan, the lender has some rights to the property. The borrower can usually claim a home equity loan as a tax deduction.

Home Inspection: an examination of the structure and mechanical systems to determine a home's quality, soundness and safety; makes the potential homebuyer aware of any repairs that may be needed. The homebuyer generally pays inspection fees.

Home Warranty: offers protection for mechanical systems and attached appliances against unexpected repairs not covered by homeowner's insurance; coverage extends over a specific time period and does not cover the home's structure.

Homeowner's Insurance: an insurance policy, also called hazard insurance, that combines protection against damage to a dwelling and its contents including fire, storms, or other damages with protection against claims of negligence or inappropriate action that result in someone's injury or property damage. Most lenders require homeowners insurance and may escrow the cost. **Flood insurance is generally not included in standard policies and must be purchased separately.**

Homeownership Education Classes: classes that stress the need to develop a strong credit history and offer information about how to get a mortgage approved, qualify for a loan, choose an affordable home, go through financing and closing processes, and avoid mortgage problems that cause people to lose their homes.

Homestead Credit: property tax credit program, offered by some state governments, that provides reductions in property taxes to eligible households.

Housing Counseling Agency: provides counseling and assistance to individuals on a variety of issues, including loan default, fair housing, and home buying.

HUD: the U.S. Department of Housing and Urban Development; established in 1965, HUD works to create a decent home and suitable living environment for all Americans; it does this by addressing housing needs, improving and developing American communities, and enforcing fair housing laws.

HUD1 Statement: also known as the "settlement sheet," or "closing statement" it itemizes all closing costs; must be given to the borrower at or before closing. Items that appear on the statement include real estate commissions, loan fees, points, and escrow amounts.

HVAC: Heating, Ventilation and Air Conditioning; a home's heating and cooling system.

I

Indemnification: to secure against any loss or damage, compensate or give security for reimbursement for loss or damage incurred. A homeowner should negotiate for inclusion of an indemnification provision in a contract with a general contractor or for a separate indemnity agreement protecting the homeowner from harm, loss or damage caused by actions or omissions of the general (and all sub) contractor.

Index: the measure of interest rate changes that the lender uses to decide how much the interest rate of an ARM will change over time. No one can be sure when an index rate will go up or down. If a lender bases interest rate adjustments on the average value of an index over time, your interest rate would not be as volatile. You should ask your lender how the index for any ARM you are considering has changed in recent years, and where it is reported.

Inflation: the number of dollars in circulation exceeds the amount of goods and services available for purchase; inflation results in a decrease in the dollar's value.

Inflation Coverage: endorsement to a homeowner's policy that automatically adjusts the amount of insurance to compensate for inflationary rises in the home's value. This type of coverage does not adjust for increases in the home's value due to improvements.

Inquiry: a credit report request. Each time a credit application is completed or more credit is requested counts as an inquiry. A large number of inquiries on a credit report can sometimes make a credit score lower.

Interest: a fee charged for the use of borrowing money.

Interest Rate: the amount of interest charged on a monthly loan payment, expressed as a percentage.

Insurance: protection against a specific loss, such as fire, wind, etc., over a period of time that is secured by the payment of a regularly scheduled premium.

J

Joint Tenancy (with Rights of Survivorship): two or more owners share equal ownership and rights to the property. If a joint owner dies, his or her share of the property passes to the other owners, without probate. In joint tenancy, ownership of the property cannot be willed to someone who is not a joint owner.

Judgment: a legal decision; when requiring debt repayment, a judgment may include a property lien that secures the creditor's claim by providing a collateral source.

Jumbo Loan: or non-conforming loan, is a loan that exceeds Fannie Mae's and Freddie Mac's loan limits. Freddie Mac and Fannie Mae loans are referred to as conforming loans.

L

Late Payment Charges: the penalty the homeowner must pay when a mortgage payment is made after the due date grace period.

Lease: a written agreement between a property owner and a tenant (resident) that stipulates the payment and conditions under which the tenant may occupy a home or apartment and states a specified period of time.

Lease Purchase (Lease Option): assists low to moderate income homebuyers in purchasing a home by allowing them to lease a home with an option to buy; the rent payment is made up of the monthly rental payment plus an additional amount that is credited to an account for use as a down payment.

Lender: A term referring to a person or company that makes loans for real estate purchases. Sometimes referred to as a loan officer or lender.

Lender Option Commitments: an agreement giving a lender the option to deliver loans or securities by a certain date at agreed-upon terms.

Liabilities: a person's financial obligations such as long-term / short-term debt, and other financial obligations to be paid.

Liability Insurance: insurance coverage that protects against claims alleging a property owner's negligence or action resulted in bodily injury or damage to another person. It is normally included in homeowner's insurance policies.

Lien: a legal claim against property that must be satisfied when the property is sold. A claim of money against a property, wherein the value of the property is used as security in repayment of a debt. Examples include a mechanic's lien, which might be for the unpaid cost of building supplies, or a tax lien for unpaid property taxes. A lien is a defect on the title and needs to be settled before transfer of ownership. A lien release is a written report of the settlement of a lien and is recorded in the public record as evidence of payment.

Lien Waiver: A document that releases a consumer (homeowner) from any further obligation for payment of a debt once it has been paid in full. Lien waivers typically are used by homeowners who hire a contractor to provide work and materials to prevent any subcontractors or suppliers of materials from filing a lien against the homeowner for nonpayment.

Life Cap: a limit on the range interest rates can increase or decrease over the life of an adjustable-rate mortgage (ARM).

Line of Credit: an agreement by a financial institution such as a bank to extend credit up to a certain amount for a certain time to a specified borrower.

Liquid Asset: a cash asset or an asset that is easily converted into cash.

Listing Agreement: a contract between a seller and a real estate professional to market and sell a home. A listing agreement obligates the real estate professional (or his or her agent) to seek qualified buyers, report all purchase offers and help negotiate the highest possible price and most favorable terms for the property seller.

Loan: money borrowed that is usually repaid with interest.

Loan Acceleration: an acceleration clause in a loan document is a statement in a mortgage that gives the lender the right to demand payment of the entire outstanding balance if a monthly payment is missed.

Loan Fraud: purposely giving incorrect information on a loan application in order to better qualify for a loan; may result in civil liability or criminal penalties.

Loan Officer: a representative of a lending or mortgage company who is responsible for soliciting homebuyers, qualifying and processing of loans. They may also be called lender, loan representative, account executive or loan rep.

Loan Origination Fee: a charge by the lender to cover the administrative costs of making the mortgage. This charge is paid at the closing and varies with the lender and type of loan. A loan origination fee of 1 to 2 % of the mortgage amount is common.

Loan Servicer: the company that collects monthly mortgage payments and disperses property taxes and insurance payments. Loan servicers also monitor nonperforming loans, contact delinquent borrowers, and notify insurers and investors of potential problems. Loan servicers may be the lender or a specialized company that just handles loan servicing under contract with the lender or the investor who owns the loan.

Loan to Value (LTV) Ratio: a percentage calculated by dividing the amount borrowed by the price or appraised value of the home to be purchased; the higher the LTV, the less cash a borrower is required to pay as down payment.

Lock-In: since interest rates can change frequently, many lenders offer an interest rate lock-in that guarantees a specific interest rate if the loan is closed within a specific time.

Lock-in Period: the length of time that the lender has guaranteed a specific interest rate to a borrower.

Loss Mitigation: a process to avoid foreclosure; the lender tries to help a borrower who has been unable to make loan payments and is in danger of defaulting on his or her loan.

M

Mandatory Delivery Commitment: an agreement that a lender will deliver loans or securities by a certain date at agreed-upon terms.

Margin: the number of percentage points the lender adds to the index rate to calculate the ARM interest rate at each adjustment.

Market Value: the amount a willing buyer would pay a willing seller for a home. An appraised value is an estimate of the current fair market value.

Maturity: the date when the principal balance of a loan becomes due and payable.

Median Price: the price of the house that falls in the middle of the total number of homes for sale in that area.

Medium Term Notes: unsecured general obligations of Fannie Mae with maturities of one day or more and with principal and interest payable in U.S. dollars.

Merged Credit Report: raw data pulled from two or more of the major credit-reporting firms.

Mitigation: term usually used to refer to various changes or improvements made in a home; for instance, to reduce the average level of radon.

Modification: when a lender agrees to modify the terms of a mortgage without refinancing the loan.

Mortgage: a lien on the property that secures the Promise to repay a loan. A security agreement between the lender and the buyer in which the property is collateral for the loan. The mortgage gives the lender the right to collect payment on the loan and to foreclose if the loan obligations are not met.

Mortgage Acceleration Clause: a clause allowing a lender, under certain circumstances, demand the entire balance of a loan is repaid in a lump sum. The acceleration clause is usually triggered if the home is sold, title to the property is changed, the loan is refinanced or the borrower defaults on a scheduled payment.

Mortgage-Backed Security (MBS): a Fannie Mae security that represents an undivided interest in a group of mortgages. Principal and interest payments from the individual mortgage loans are grouped and paid out to the MBS holders.

Mortgage Banker: a company that originates loans and resells them to secondary mortgage lenders like Fannie Mae or Freddie Mac.

Mortgage Broker: a firm that originates and processes loans for a number of lenders.

Mortgage Life and Disability Insurance: term life insurance bought by borrowers to pay off a mortgage in the event of death or make monthly payments in the case of disability. The amount of coverage decreases as the principal balance declines. There are many different terms of coverage determining amounts of payments and when payments begin and end.

Mortgage Insurance: a policy that protects lenders against some or most of the losses that can occur when a borrower defaults on a mortgage loan; mortgage insurance is required primarily for borrowers with a down payment of less than 20% of the home's purchase price. Insurance purchased by the buyer to protect the lender in the event of default. Typically purchased for loans with less than 20 % down payment. The cost of mortgage insurance is usually added to the monthly payment. Mortgage insurance is maintained on conventional loans until the outstanding amount of the loan is less than 80 % of the value of the house or for a set period of time (7 years is common). Mortgage insurance also is available through a government agency, such as the Federal Housing Administration (FHA) or through companies (Private Mortgage Insurance or PMI).

Mortgage Insurance Premium (MIP): a monthly payment—usually part of the mortgage payment—paid by a borrower for mortgage insurance.

Mortgage Interest Deduction: the interest cost of a mortgage, which is a tax- deductible expense. The interest reduces the taxable income of taxpayers.

Mortgage Modification: a loss mitigation option that allows a borrower to refinance and/or extend the term of the mortgage loan and thus reduce the monthly payments.

Mortgage Note: a legal document obligating a borrower to repay a loan at a stated interest rate during a specified period; the agreement is secured by a mortgage that is recorded in the public records along with the deed.

Mortgage Qualifying Ratio: Used to calculate the maximum amount of funds that an individual traditionally may be able to afford. A typical mortgage qualifying ratio is 28: 36.

Mortgage Score: a score based on a combination of information about the borrower that is obtained from the loan application, the credit report, and property value information. The score is a comprehensive analysis of the borrower's ability to repay a mortgage loan and manage credit.

Mortgagee: the lender in a mortgage agreement.

Mortgagor: the borrower in a mortgage agreement.

Multifamily Housing: a building with more than four residential rental units.

Multiple Listing Service (MLS): Realtors submit listings and agree to attempt to sell all properties in the MLS. The MLS is a service of the local Board of Realtors®. The local MLS has a protocol for updating listings and sharing commissions. The MLS offers the advantage of more timely information, availability, and access to houses and other types of property on the market.

N

National Credit Repositories: currently, there are three companies that maintain national credit-reporting databases. These are Equifax, Experian, and Trans Union, referred to as Credit Bureaus.

Negative Amortization: amortization means that monthly payments are large enough to pay the interest and reduce the principal on your mortgage. Negative amortization occurs when the monthly payments do not cover all of the interest cost. The interest cost that isn't covered is added to the unpaid principal balance. This means that even after making many payments, you could owe more than you did at the beginning of the loan. Negative amortization can occur when an ARM has a payment cap that results in monthly payments not high enough to cover the interest due.

Net Income: Your take-home pay, the amount of money that you receive in your paycheck after taxes and deductions.

No Cash Out Refinance: a refinance of an existing loan only for the amount remaining on the mortgage. The borrower does not get any cash against the equity of the home. Also called a "rate and term refinance."

No Cost Loan: there are many variations of a no cost loan. Generally, it is a loan that does not charge for items such as title insurance, escrow fees, settlement fees, appraisal, recording fees, or notary fees. It may also offer no points. This lessens the need for upfront cash during the buying process however no cost loans have a higher interest rate.

Nonperforming Asset: an asset such as a mortgage that is not currently accruing interest or which interest is not being paid.

Note: a legal document obligating a borrower to repay a mortgage loan at a stated interest rate over a specified period of time.

Note Rate: the interest rate stated on a mortgage note.

Notice of Default: a formal written notice to a borrower that there is a default on a loan and that legal action is possible.

Non-Conforming Loan: is a loan that exceeds Fannie Mae's and Freddie Mac's loan limits. Freddie Mac and Fannie Mae loans are referred to as conforming loans.

Notary Public: a person who serves as a public official and certifies the authenticity of required signatures on a document by signing and stamping the document.

O

Offer: indication by a potential buyer of a willingness to purchase a home at a specific price; generally put forth in writing.

Original Principal Balance: the total principal owed on a mortgage prior to any payments being made.

Origination: the process of preparing, submitting, and evaluating a loan application; generally includes a credit check, verification of employment, and a property appraisal.

Origination Fee: the charge for originating a loan; is usually calculated in the form of points and paid at closing. One point equals 1% of the loan amount. On a conventional loan, the loan origination fee is the number of points a borrower pays.

Owner Financing: a home purchase where the seller provides all or part of the financing, acting as a lender.

Ownership: ownership is documented by the deed to a property. The type or form of ownership is important if there is a change in the status of the owners or if the property changes ownership.

Owner's Policy: the insurance policy that protects the buyer from title defects.

P

PITI: Principal, Interest, Taxes, and Insurance: the four elements of a monthly mortgage payment; payments of principal and interest go directly toward repaying the loan while the portion that covers taxes and insurance (homeowner's and mortgage, if applicable) goes into an escrow account to cover the fees when they are due.

PITI Reserves: a cash amount that a borrower must have on hand after making a down payment and paying all closing costs for the purchase of a home. The principal, interest, taxes, and insurance (PITI) reserves must equal the amount that the borrower would have to pay for PITI for a predefined number of months.

PMI: Private Mortgage Insurance; privately owned companies that offer standard and special affordable mortgage insurance programs for qualified borrowers with down payments of less than 20% of a purchase price.

Partial Payment: a payment that is less than the total amount owed on a monthly mortgage payment. Normally, lenders do not accept partial payments. The lender may make exceptions during times of difficulty. Contact your lender prior to the due date if a partial payment is needed.

Payment Cap: a limit on how much an ARM;s payment may increase, regardless of how much the interest rate increases.

Payment Change Date: the date when a new monthly payment amount takes effect on an adjustable-rate mortgage (ARM) or a graduated-payment mortgage (GPM). Generally, the payment change date occurs in the month immediately after the interest rate adjustment date.

Payment Due Date: Contract language specifying when payments are due on money borrowed. The due date is always indicated and means that the payment must be received on or before the specified date. Grace periods prior to assessing a late fee or additional interest do not eliminate the responsibility of making payments on time.

Perils: for homeowner's insurance, an event that can damage the property. Homeowner's insurance may cover the property for a wide variety of perils caused by accidents, nature, or people.

Personal Property: any property that is not real property or attached to real property. For example, furniture is not attached; however, a new light fixture would be considered attached and part of the real property.

Planned Unit Development (PUD): a development that is planned and constructed as one entity. Generally, there are common features in the homes or lots governed by covenants attached to the deed. Most planned developments have common land and facilities owned and managed by the owner's or neighborhood association. Homeowners usually are required to participate in the association via a payment of annual dues.

Points: a point is equal to one percent of the principal amount of your mortgage. For example, if you get a mortgage for $95,000, one point means you pay $950 to the lender. Lenders frequently charge points in both fixed-rate and adjustable-rate mortgages in order to increase the yield on the mortgage and to cover loan closing costs. These points usually are collected at closing and may be paid by the borrower or the home seller, or may be split between them.

Power of Attorney: a legal document that authorizes another person to act on your behalf. A power of attorney can grant complete authority or can be limited to certain acts or certain periods of time or both.

Pre-Approval: a lender commits to lend to a potential borrower a fixed loan amount based on a completed loan application, credit reports, debt, savings and has been reviewed by an underwriter. The commitment remains as long as the borrower still meets the qualification requirements at the time of purchase. This does not guarantee a loan until the property has passed inspections underwriting guidelines.

Predatory Lending: abusive lending practices that include a mortgage loan to someone who does not have the ability to repay. It also pertains to repeated refinancing of a loan charging high interest and fees each time.

Predictive Variables: the variables that are part of the formula comprising elements of a credit-scoring model. These variables are used to predict a borrower's future credit performance.

Preferred Stock: stock that takes priority over common stock with regard to dividends and liquidation rights. Preferred stockholders typically have no voting rights.

Pre-foreclosure Sale: a procedure in which the borrower is allowed to sell a property for an amount less than what is owed on it to avoid a foreclosure. This sale fully satisfies the borrower's debt.

Pre-Qualify: a lender informally determines the maximum amount an individual is eligible to borrow. This is not a guarantee of a loan.

Premium: an amount paid on a regular schedule by a policyholder that maintains insurance coverage.

Prepayment: payment of the mortgage loan before the scheduled due date; may be subject to a prepayment penalty.

Prepayment Penalty: a fee charged to a homeowner who pays one or more monthly payments before the due date. It can also apply to principal-reduction payments.

Prepayment Penalty Mortgage (PPM): a type of mortgage that requires the borrower to pay a penalty for prepayment, partial payment of principal or for repaying the entire loan within a certain time period. A partial payment is generally defined as an amount exceeding 20% of the original principal balance.

Price Range: the high and low amount a buyer is willing to pay for a home.

Prime Rate: the interest rate that banks charge to preferred customers. Changes in the prime rate are publicized in the business media. Prime rate can be used as the basis for adjustable rate mortgages (ARMs) or home equity lines of credit. The prime rate also affects the current interest rates being offered at a particular point in time on fixed mortgages. Changes in the prime rate do not affect the interest on a fixed mortgage.

Principal: the amount of money borrowed to buy a house or the amount of the loan that has not been paid back to the lender. This does not include the interest paid to borrow that money. The principal balance is the amount owed on a loan at any given time. It is the original loan amount minus the total repayments of principal made.

Principal, Interest, Taxes, and Insurance (PITI): the four elements of a monthly mortgage payment; payments of principal and interest go directly toward repaying the loan while the portion that covers taxes and insurance (homeowner's and mortgage, if applicable) goes into an escrow account to cover the fees when they are due.

Private Mortgage Insurance (PMI): insurance purchased by a buyer to protect the lender in the event of default. The cost of mortgage insurance is usually added to the monthly payment. Mortgage insurance is generally maintained until over 20 Percent of the outstanding amount of the loan is paid or for a set period of time, seven years is normal. Mortgage insurance may be available through a government agency, such as the Federal Housing Administration (FHA) or the Veterans Administration (VA), or through private mortgage insurance companies (PMI).

Promissory Note: a written promise to repay a specified amount over a specified period of time.

Property (Fixture and Non-Fixture): in a real estate contract, the property is the land within the legally described boundaries and all permanent structures and fixtures. Ownership of the property confers the legal right to use the property as allowed within the law and within the restrictions of zoning or easements. Fixture property refers to those items permanently attached to the structure, such as carpeting or a ceiling fan, which transfers with the property.

Property Tax: a tax charged by local government and used to fund municipal services such as schools, police, or street maintenance. The amount of property tax is determined locally by a formula, usually based on a percent per $1,000 of assessed value of the property.

Property Tax Deduction: the U.S. tax code allows homeowners to deduct the amount they have paid in property taxes from their total income.

Public Record Information: Court records of events that are a matter of public interest such as credit, bankruptcy, foreclosure and tax liens. The presence of public record information on a credit report is regarded negatively by creditors.

Punch List: a list of items that have not been completed at the time of the final walk- through of a newly constructed home.

Purchase Offer: A detailed, written document that makes an offer to purchase a property, and that may be amended several times in the process of negotiations. When signed by all parties involved in the sale, the purchase offer becomes a legally binding contract, sometimes called the Sales Contract.

Q

Qualifying Ratios: guidelines utilized by lenders to determine how much money a homebuyer is qualified to borrow. Lending guidelines typically include a maximum housing expense to income ratio and a maximum monthly expense to income ratio.

Quitclaim Deed: a deed transferring ownership of a property but does not make any guarantee of clear title.

R

RESPA: Real Estate Settlement Procedures Act; a law protecting consumers from abuses during the residential real estate purchase and loan process by requiring lenders to disclose all settlement costs, practices, and relationships

Radon: a radioactive gas found in some homes that, if occurring in strong enough concentrations, can cause health problems.

Rate Cap: a limit on an ARM on how much the interest rate or mortgage payment may change. Rate caps limit how much the interest rates can rise or fall on the adjustment dates and over the life of the loan.

Rate Lock: a commitment by a lender to a borrower guaranteeing a specific interest rate over a period of time at a set cost.

Real Estate Agent: an individual who is licensed to negotiate and arrange real estate sales; works for a real estate broker.

Real Estate Mortgage Investment Conduit (REMIC): a security representing an interest in a trust having multiple classes of securities. The securities of each class entitle investors to cash payments structured differently from the payments on the underlying mortgages.

Real Estate Property Tax Deduction: a tax deductible expense reducing a taxpayer's taxable income.

Real Estate Settlement Procedures Act (RESPA): a law protecting consumers from abuses during the residential real estate purchase and loan process by requiring lenders to disclose all settlement costs, practices, and relationships

Real Property: land, including all the natural resources and permanent buildings on it.

REALTOR®: a real estate agent or broker who is a member of the NATIONAL ASSOCIATION OF REALTORS, and its local and state associations.

Recorder: the public official who keeps records of transactions concerning real property. Sometimes known as a "Registrar of Deeds" or "County Clerk."

Recording: the recording in a registrar's office of an executed legal document. These include deeds, mortgages, satisfaction of a mortgage, or an extension of a mortgage making it a part of the public record.

Recording Fees: charges for recording a deed with the appropriate government agency.

Refinancing: paying off one loan by obtaining another; refinancing is generally done to secure better loan terms (like a lower interest rate).

Rehabilitation Mortgage: a mortgage that covers the costs of rehabilitating (repairing or Improving) a property; some rehabilitation mortgages—like the FHA's 203(k)—allow a borrower to roll the costs of rehabilitation and home purchase into one mortgage loan.

Reinstatement Period: a phase of the foreclosure process where the homeowner has an opportunity to stop the foreclosure by paying money that is owed to the lender.

Remaining Balance: the amount of principal that has not yet been repaid.

Remaining Term: the original amortization term minus the number of payments that have been applied.

Repayment plan: an agreement between a lender and a delinquent borrower where the borrower agrees to make additional payments to pay down past due amounts while making regularly scheduled payments.

Return On Average Common Equity: net income available to common stockholders, as a percentage of average common stockholder equity.

Reverse Mortgage (HECM): the reverse mortgage is used by senior homeowners age 62 and older to convert the equity in their home into monthly streams of income and/or a line of credit to be repaid when they no longer occupy the home. A lending institution such as a mortgage lender, bank, credit union or savings and loan association funds the FHA insured loan, commonly known as HECM.

Right of First Refusal: a provision in an agreement that requires the owner of a property to give one party an opportunity to purchase or lease a property before it is offered for sale or lease to others.

S

Sale Leaseback: when a seller deeds property to a buyer for a payment, and the buyer simultaneously leases the property back to the seller.

Second Mortgage: an additional mortgage on property. In case of a default the first mortgage must be paid before the second mortgage. Second loans are more risky for the lender and usually carry a higher interest rate.

Secondary Mortgage Market: the buying and selling of mortgage loans. Investors purchase residential mortgages originated by lenders, which in turn provides the lenders with capital for additional lending.

Secured Loan: a loan backed by collateral such as property.

Security: the property that will be pledged as collateral for a loan.

Seller Carry Back/Seller Financing: an agreement where the owner of a property provides second mortgage financing. These are often combined with an assumed mortgage instead of a portion of the seller's equity.

Serious Delinquency: a mortgage that is 90 days or more past due.

Servicer: a business that collects mortgage payments from borrowers and manages the borrower's escrow accounts.

Servicing: the collection of mortgage payments from borrowers and related responsibilities of a loan servicer.

Setback: the distance between a property line and the area where building can take place. Setbacks are used to assure space between buildings and from roads for a many of purposes including drainage and utilities.

Settlement: another name for closing.

Settlement Statement: a document required by the Real Estate Settlement Procedures Act (RESPA). It is an itemized statement of services and charges relating to the closing of a property transfer. The buyer has the right to examine the settlement statement one day before the closing. This is called the HUD 1 Settlement Statement.

Sub-Prime Loan: "B" Loan or "B" paper with FICO scores from 620—659. "C" Loan or C" Paper with FICO scores typically from 580–619. An industry term to used to describe loans with less stringent lending and underwriting terms and conditions. Due to the higher risk, sub-prime loans charge higher interest rates and fees.

Subordinate: to place in a rank of lesser importance or to make one claim secondary to another.

Survey: a property diagram that indicates legal boundaries, easements, encroachments, rights of way, improvement locations, etc. Surveys are conducted by licensed surveyors and are normally required by the lender in order to confirm that the property boundaries and features such as buildings, and easements are correctly described in the legal description of the property.

Sweat Equity: using labor to build or improve a property as part of the down payment.

T

Third Party Origination: a process by which a lender uses another party to completely or partially originate, process, underwrite, close, fund, or package the mortgages it plans to deliver to the secondary mortgage market.

Terms: the period of time and the interest rate agreed upon by the lender and the borrower to repay a loan.

Title: a legal document establishing the right of ownership and is recorded to make it part of the public record. Also known as a Deed.

Title 1: an FHA-insured loan that allows a borrower to make non-luxury improvements (like renovations or repairs) to their home; Title I loans less than $7,500 don't require a property lien.

Title Company: a company that specializes in examining and insuring titles to real estate.

Title Defect: an outstanding claim on a property that limits the ability to sell the property. Also referred to as a cloud on the title.

Title Insurance: insurance that protects the lender against any claims that arise from arguments about ownership of the property; also available for homebuyers. An insurance policy guaranteeing the accuracy of a title search protecting against errors. Most lenders require the buyer to purchase title insurance protecting the lender against loss in the event of a title defect. This charge is included in the closing costs. A policy that protects the buyer from title defects is known as an owner's policy and requires an additional charge.

Title Search: a check of public records to be sure that the seller is the recognized owner of the real estate and that there are no unsettled liens or other claims against the property.

Transfer Agent: a bank or trust company charged with keeping a record of a company's stockholders and canceling and issuing certificates as shares are bought and sold.

Transfer of Ownership: any means by which ownership of a property changes hands. These include purchase of a property, assumption of mortgage debt, exchange of possession of a property via a land sales contract or any other land trust device.

Transfer Taxes: State and local taxes charged for the transfer of real estate. Usually equal to a percentage of the sales price.

Treasury Index: can be used as the basis for adjustable rate mortgages (ARMs) It is based on the results of auctions that the U.S. Treasury holds for its Treasury bills and securities.

Truth-in-Lending: a federal law obligating a lender to give full written disclosure of all fees, terms, and conditions associated with the loan initial period and then adjusts to another rate that lasts for the term of the loan.

Two Step Mortgage: an adjustable-rate mortgage (ARM) that has one interest rate for the first five to seven years of its term and a different interest rate for the remainder of the term.

Trustee: a person who holds or controls property for the benefit of another.

U

Underwriting: the process of analyzing a loan application to determine the amount of risk involved in making the loan; it includes a review of the potential borrower's credit history and a judgment of the property value.

Up-Front Charges: the fees charged to homeowners by the lender at the time of closing a mortgage loan. This includes points, brokers fees, insurance, and other charges.

V

VA (Department of Veterans Affairs): a federal agency that guarantees loans made to veterans; similar to mortgage insurance, a loan guarantee protects lenders against loss that may result from a borrower default.

VA Mortgage: a mortgage guaranteed by the Department of Veterans Affairs (VA).

Variable Expenses: Costs or payments that may vary from month to month, for example, gasoline or food.

Variance: a special exemption of a zoning law to allow the property to be used in a manner different from an existing law.

Vested: a point in time when you may withdraw funds from an investment account, such as a retirement account, without penalty.

W

Walk-Through: the final inspection of a property being sold by the buyer to confirm that any contingencies specified in the purchase agreement such as repairs have been completed, fixture and non-fixture property is in place and confirm the electrical, mechanical, and plumbing systems are in working order.

Warranty Deed: a legal document that includes the guarantee the seller is the true owner of the property, has the right to sell the property, and there are no claims against the property.

X ,Y, Z

Zoning: local laws established to control the uses of land within a particular area. Zoning laws are used to separate residential land from areas of non-residential use, such as industry or businesses. Zoning ordinances include many provisions governing such things as type of structure, setbacks, lot size, and uses of a building.

Source: Information provided by the Department of Housing and Urban Development.

INDEX

ABOUT THE AUTHOR

During his 30 years as a real estate broker, H. Richard Steinhoff has been involved in thousands of transactions with buyers and sellers. This gives him a unique perspective, because he can speak from experience "in the trenches."

Richard's education includes a Bachelor of Science degree in Business Administration from California State University, and a Certificate in Business from UCLA Graduate School of Business.

His real estate background includes serving as president of the ERA Broker Council, president of the Broker Council of Southern California, vice-president and director of the Board of Realtors, director of the California Association of Realtors, and member of the National Association of Realtors.

Richard's community involvement has included serving as vice-president and director of the Chamber of Commerce, president of Center 500 (a major fundraising organization for the for the Segerstrom Center for the Arts), ex-officio director of the Segerstrom Center for the Arts, director of the Laguna Niguel Community Council, president of the Club at Rancho Niguel, and president of the Crown Royale Homeowners' Association.

He has received the "Man of the Year" Award from the Chamber of Commerce, the President's Award from the Muscular Dystrophy Association, and has been listed in *"Who's Who in California"* as well as *"Who's Who in the West."* Richard holds a CIBM designation and is a member of the American Mensa Society.

He is an avid golfer, amateur magician, and a U.S. Marine Corps veteran.

Richard lives in Laguna Niguel, California, with his wife, Elaine. They have 4 children, and 10 grandchildren.

FREE BONUS GIFTS

As a thank-you for purchasing *Turning Myths into Money: An Insider's Guide to Winning the Real Estate Game*, H. Richard Steinhoff is offering you the following free gifts:

- **Finding the Best Mortgage**

  A report to assist you in obtaining the best mortgage for your situation, including a two page Mortgage Shopping Worksheet.

- **Buying and Financing a Home**

  A report covering all aspects of buying and financing a home, including a detailed explanation of settlement (closing) costs and settlement (closing) statements.

  This report is invaluable to potential homebuyers.

- **99 Questions and Answers About Buying a Home**

  This extensive report will answer just about any question you might have about buying a home including getting started, finding your home, general financing, and closing.

  Every potential homebuyer should read this report before shopping for a home.

To claim your free gifts, go to:

www.hrichardsteinhoff.com/getyourbonus.html

BUY A SHARE OF THE FUTURE IN YOUR COMMUNITY

These certificates make great holiday, graduation and birthday gifts that can be personalized with the recipient's name. The cost of one S.H.A.R.E. or one square foot is $54.17. The personalized certificate is suitable for framing and will state the number of shares purchased and the amount of each share, as well as the recipient's name. The home that you participate in "building" will last for many years and will continue to grow in value.

Here is a sample SHARE certificate:

HABITAT FOR HUMANITY

THIS CERTIFIES THAT

YOUR NAME HERE

HAS INVESTED IN A HOME FOR A DESERVING FAMILY

1985-2010

TWENTY-FIVE YEARS OF BUILDING FUTURES
IN OUR COMMUNITY ONE HOME AT A TIME

1200 SQUARE FOOT HOUSE @ $65,000 = $54.17 PER SQUARE FOOT
This certificate represents a tax deductible donation. It has no cash value.

YES, I WOULD LIKE TO HELP!

I support the work that Habitat for Humanity does and I want to be part of the excitement! As a donor, I will receive periodic updates on your construction activities but, more importantly, I know my gift will help a family in our community realize the dream of homeownership. **I would like to SHARE in your efforts against substandard housing in my community!** *(Please print below)*

PLEASE SEND ME _____ SHARES at $54.17 EACH = $ $_____

In Honor Of: _____

Occasion: (Circle One)   HOLIDAY   BIRTHDAY   ANNIVERSARY

    OTHER: _____

Address of Recipient: _____

Gift From: _____ *Donor Address:* _____

Donor Email: _____

I AM ENCLOSING A CHECK FOR $ $_____ PAYABLE TO HABITAT FOR HUMANITY <u>OR</u> PLEASE CHARGE MY VISA OR MASTERCARD *(CIRCLE ONE)*

Card Number _____ Expiration Date: _____

Name as it appears on Credit Card _____ Charge Amount $ _____

Signature _____

Billing Address _____

Telephone # Day _____ Eve _____

PLEASE NOTE: Your contribution is tax-deductible to the fullest extent allowed by law.
Habitat for Humanity • P.O. Box 1443 • Newport News, VA 23601 • 757-596-5553
www.HelpHabitatforHumanity.org

Printed in the USA
CPSIA information can be obtained
at www.ICGtesting.com
JSHW082201140824
68134JS00014B/369